엄마표 생활영어 레시피

How are you? Fine. Thank you.
And you? 이제 그만!

엄마표 생활영어 레시피_훈육 편

초판 1쇄 발행 2022년 1월 29일
초판 2쇄 발행 2022년 2월 10일

지은이 반두레(시온맘)

대표 장선희 **총괄** 이영철
기획편집 이소정, 정시아, 한이슬, 현미나
디자인 김효숙, 최아영 **외주디자인** 이창욱
마케팅 최의범, 강주영, 김현진, 이동희
경영관리 문경국
본문 일러스트 복치

펴낸곳 서사원 **출판등록** 제2021-000194호
주소 서울시 영등포구 당산로 54길 11 상가 301호
전화 02-898-8778 **팩스** 02-6008-1673
이메일 cr@seosawon.com
블로그 blog.naver.com/seosawon
페이스북 www.facebook.com/seosawon
인스타그램 www.instagram.com/seosawon

ISBN 979-11-6822-042-3 13740

서사원은 독자 여러분의 책에 관한 아이디어와 원고 투고를 설레는 마음으로 기다리고 있습니다. 책으로 엮기를 원하는 아이디어가 있는 분은 이메일 cr@seosawon.com으로 간단한 개요와 취지, 연락처 등을 보내주세요. 고민을 멈추고 실행해보세요. 꿈이 이루어집니다.

엄마표 생활영어 레시피

How are you? Fine. Thank you. And you? 이제 그만!

훈육편

반두레(시온맘) 지음

서사원

프롤로그

이중언어! 인풋의 방식과 비율 이전에 언어 사용자와의 관계성이 아이의 아웃풋과 더 밀접한 관련이 있음을 절감하고 있습니다

이제 막 돌이 지난 아들에게 엄마표 이중언어를 실천하고자 마음먹었던 때가 떠오릅니다. 당시 남편은 해외 근무로 곁에 없었고, 육아에 양가 찬스는 꿈도 꿀 수 없었던 시점이었습니다. 설상가상으로 코로나19까지 터지면서 아이는 다니던 어린이집도 그만두게 되었어요.

처음 말을 배우기 시작한 아이에게 언어의 인풋은 모두 엄마의 몫이 되었습니다. 그러니 엄마표 이중언어에 대해 고민하지 않을 수 없었어요. 조언자를 찾아야 했습니다. 엄마표 이중언어에 대한 사례와 맞다 틀리다에 관한 여러 가지 주장들은 많았습니다.

하지만 하루가 다르게 자라는 내 아이에게 시기마다 적절하게 적용할 구체적인 방법을 얻을 수가 없었어요. 그래서 언어 교육에 대한 서적들을 읽으며 엄마인 나는 어떻게 외국어를 습득할 수 있었나 되돌아보았습니다. 그리고 내 아이는 어떤 성향인가를 관찰했습니다.

가정 보육을 하는 동안, 아이의 언어가 폭발적으로 발달하기 시작했습니다. 한국어와 영어 모두 의사소통이 어렵지 않은 단계가 되었어요. 스스로도 신기해서 아이의 언어 발달과 엄마의 지혜를 글과 영상으로 남기기 시작했습니다.

제 아이를 위해 시작한 엄마표 영어가 자연스럽게 저의 콘텐츠가 되었고, SNS라는 공간에서 아버님 어머님들과 소통의 도구가 되었습니다. 아빠표, 엄마표 영어를 실천하고 계신 부모님들의 고충을 듣게 되면서 도움을 드리고 싶어졌어요. 제가 할 수 있는 일들이 보였고, 즐거웠습니다. 아이와 핑퐁 대화가 가능해지면서, 육아 영어 서적들의 아쉬운 점을 발견했습니다.

일상에서 시온이와 나누던 대화 내용들을 정리하기 시작했어요. 이것이 자료가 되었고 나눔으로 이어지게 되었습니다. 그런데 몇몇 분들이 나눔한 자료를 판매하거나 재배포를 하는 바람에 저는 자료를 지켜야 했습니다. 그러던 차에 출판사의 제안으로 자연스럽게 책이 만들어지게 되었어요. 분량은 가독성과 실현 가능성 등을 고려해 처음 원고의 1/4로 줄였습니다. 고민하고 선별하여 훈육 파트만 1권으로 담아냈습니다. 2권은 독자 분들의 관심과 니즈에 따라 이어지지 않을까 생각해 봅니다.

이중언어를 실천하며 진지하게 고민했던 내용을 책에 담았습니다. 특히 아이가 속상한 감정을 외국어로 표현했을 때, 부모가 아이의 언어로 마음을 달래줄 수 있는 준비가 잘 되어 있어야 한다는 깨달음이 가장 절실했습니다. 인풋의 방식과 비율 이전에, 언어 사용자와의 관계성이 아웃풋에 매우 중요한 영향을 끼치는 경험을 했기 때문입니다.

SNS에서 엄마표 영어 콘텐츠를 다루며, 시온이 할머니 이야기를 공유하는 저변에는 부모와 자녀의 관계를 강조하고 싶은 시온이 엄마의 마음이 숨어 있습니다. 이 책에는 저의 그런 마음들이 담겨 있어요. 가정에서 아이와 함께 생활영어를 실천하고 계신 부모님들께 작은 도움이 되길 바랍니다.

부모의 영어 공부와 부모표 영어는 매우 다르다고 생각합니다. 전자는 부모를 위한 학습이 되지만, 후자는 부모는 물론 아이를 위한 학습이 됩니다. 영화 대본, 영어 도서 및 낭독, 뉴스 및 기사 외우기, 토익, 토플, 텝스, 아이엘츠 등의 시험보기 모두 다 좋지만, 부모표 영어는 자라는 아이의 상황을 고려해 주어야 한다고 생각해요. 아빠 또는 엄마의 영어 수준과 관계없이 먼저는 부모표 생활영어를 실천해 보시라고 권하고 싶습니다. 제가 생각하는 아빠표 영어 엄마표 영어는 그렇습니다.

시온이네 콘텐츠를 따뜻한 시선으로 바라봐 주시고, 공감하며 소통해 주시는 구독자 분들께 감사의 마음을 전합니다. 마음을 전해주시는 분들이 계셔서 꾸준히 나누게 됩니다. 자료가 책이 될 수 있었던 이유도 여기에 있습니다. 감사합니다.

자료 나눔에 함께해주신 신혜조 선생님, 진심으로 감사드립니다. 혼자가 아니라서 즐겁게 준비할 수 있었습니다. 멋진 목소리로 자료를 소개해주신 크리에이터 준호씨, 고마운 마음 전합니다. 원고 작업에 도움을 주신 Robin 선생님, 감사합니다. 고생 많으셨습니다. 외로운 시간을 잘 견뎌낼 수 있도록 친구가 되어주신 신동엽 사장님, 강경민 사장님, 고맙습니다. 덕분에 정말 재밌었습니다. 부족한 아내를 항상 기다려주고 지원해 주는 남편, 사랑합니다.

시온맘 드림

《엄마표 생활영어 레시피》 사용설명서

● 파란색 괄호 안에 플러스와 함께 정리된 내용은 아래 검정색으로 정리된 문장들 앞에 더할 수 있는 표현들입니다. 검정색으로 정리된 문장들만 사용하셔도 의미는 동일하게 전달됩니다.

시온맘's Pick

"Why don't you turn it off now?"

다양하게 표현할 수 있어요!

(+ Why don't you - ?)

Turn off the TV (now).

(Why don't you - ?)

Let's turn it off (now).
the TV

It's time to turn it off.
the TV.

● 문장에서 노란색 하이라이트 된 자리는 아래로 나란히 나열된 표현들이 대신할 수 있습니다.

● 파란색 괄호 안에 플러스 없이 정리된 내용은 아래 파란색 하이라이트 된 부분을 지우고 대신할 수 있는 표현들입니다.

하이라이트 된 자리는 아래로 나란히 나열된 표현들이 대신할 수 있습니다.

시온맘's Pick

"Throwing is not a right thing to do."

다양하게 표현할 수 있어요!

No throwing!

Throwing is not nice.
right.

You should not throw things.

Throwing is not a nice thing to do.
right

* 아래 두 문장은 매우 단호한 표현입니다.

* Throwing is not allowed.
acceptable.

노란색으로 하이라이트 된 자리
빨간색으로 하이라이트 된 자리
모두 동일합니다.

시온맘's Pick

"Let's hug one another and share our feelings."

다양하게 표현할 수 있어요!

Let's hug. + *
Let's hug each other. + *
Let's hug one another. + *
Let's give each other a hug. + *

* and talk it out.
* and have a talk.
* and talk about it.
* and share our feelings.
* and discuss what happened.
* and talk about what happened.

Let's hug and talk together.

● 핑크색 별 표시와 함께 정리된 표현들은 원하시는 대로 자유롭게 골라, 핑크색 플러스 뒤에 더하세요.

시온맘's Pick

"Don't give up here."

다양하게 표현할 수 있어요!

(+ Please)
Don't give up (now / here).

● 괄호는 생략 가능하며, 괄호 안에 표현이 두 개 이상일 경우, 선택하세요.

시온맘's Pick

"I'm sorry. Don't stay angry at me."

다양하게 표현할 수 있어요!

I'm sorry. I want you to feel better.

I'm sorry. (Please) Don't stay mad at me.
angry

I'm sorry. (Please) Stop being mad at me.

● 괄호는 생략 가능합니다.

시온맘's Pick

"If you talk like that, she might be upset."

이렇게도 표현할 수 있어요!

(may be / might be / can be / could be)
(may feel / might feel / can feel / could feel)

● 파란색으로 추가 정리된 표현들은 문장 안에 파란색 표현을 대신할 수 있습니다.

He may feel sad, if you speak that way.
She bad,
Your friend mad,
upset,

If you say it like that, he may feel sad.
talk she bad.
speak mad.
pset.

차례

Table of Contents

전개
Beginning

부르기

Calling Them

이야기 나누게 가까이 와보렴

시온맘's Pick

"Come this way so we can talk."

다양하게 표현할 수 있어요!

Come and talk to me.
Come this way so we can talk.
Come closer so that we can have a talk.

이쪽으로 와보렴

시온맘's Pick

"Get yourself over here."

다양하게 표현할 수 있어요!

Come here.
Come closer.
Come this way.
Come over here.
Come right here.
Get yourself over here.
Bring yourself over here.

시온맘's Pick

"Why don't you get yourself over here?"

이렇게도 표현할 수 있어요!

(+ Won't you - ?)
(+ Why don't you - ?)

Come here.
Come closer.
Come this way.
Come over here.
Come right here.
Get yourself over here.
Bring yourself over here.

* 여러 차례 불러도 오지 않는 경우, 위 문장들 전에 아래 표현들 중 하나를 더해주시면 조금 더 단호한 느낌이 납니다.

* I'm asking you to -
* I've asked you to -
* I've already told you to -
* I've already asked you to -

시온맘's Pick

"I've already told you to get yourself over here."

* 여러 차례 불러도 오지 않는 경우, 위 문장들 전이나 후에 아래 표현들 중 하나를 더해주시면 조금 더 단호한 느낌이 납니다.

* I won't ask (you) twice.
* I won't ask (you) again.

시온맘's Pick

"Get yourself over here. I won't ask twice."

안아주기

Giving Them a Hug

엄마가 안아줄게, 이리 와봐

시온맘's Pick

"Bring it in."

다양하게 표현할 수 있어요!

Bring it in.

Let me hug you.
mommy

Let me give you a hug.
mommy

Let me hold you.
mommy

I will give you a hug.
Mommy

* 엄마가 아이에게 자신을 표현하는 경우, 문장의 주어 또는 목적어로 I, Me, Mom보다는 Mommy를 더 많이 사용합니다. 더 친근한 느낌을 담고 있기 때문입니다.
* 위 문장들 전이나 후에 아래 표현들 중 하나를 더할 수 있습니다.

* Come here.
* Come closer.
* Come this way.

시온맘's Pick

"Come this way. Bring it in."

엄마가 꼭 안아줄게

시온맘's Pick

"I'll give you a big bear hug."

다양하게 표현할 수 있어요!

Can I give you a hug?

I'll hug you tight.
hold

I'll give you a hug.
a big hug.
a bear hug.
a big bear hug.
my biggest hug.

시온맘's Pick

"Let me give you a big bear hug."

이렇게도 표현할 수 있어요!

(Let me -)
(I want to -)
I'll hug you tight.
hold

I'll give you a hug.
a big hug.
a bear hug.
a big bear hug.
my biggest hug.

가까이 와서 엄마 품에 안기렴

시온맘's Pick

"Cuddle close. Scooch in a little closer."

다양하게 표현할 수 있어요!

Come closer, into my arms.

Cuddle close. Scooch in.
in closer.
in a little closer.

와서 엄마 안아줘

시온맘's Pick

"Come hug mommy."

다양하게 표현할 수 있어요!

Bring it in.

Give me a hug.
mommy

Let me hug you.
mommy

Let me hold you.
mommy

Let me give you a hug.
mommy

Come (and) hug me.
mommy.

Come and give me a hug.
mommy

* 엄마가 아이에게 자신을 표현하는 경우, 문장의 목적어로 Me와 Mom보다는 Mommy를 더 많이 사용합니다. 더 친근한 느낌을 담고 있기 때문입니다.

엄마 꼬옥 안아줘

시온맘's Pick

"Can you give me a bear hug?"

다양하게 표현할 수 있어요!

(+ Please 안 됨)

Bear hugs!

(+ Please)

Hug me tight.
Hold

Give me a big hug.
your biggest hug.

Come and squeeze me tight.

(+ Please 안 됨)

I want you to hug me tight.
hold

Can you give me a big hug?
bear
big bear

엄마랑 같이 이야기해보자

시온맘's Pick

"Let's share our feelings."

다양하게 표현할 수 있어요!

Let's talk it out.
Let's have a talk.
Let's talk about it.
Let's share our feelings.
Let's discuss what happened.
Let's talk about what happened.

시온맘's Pick

"Why don't we share our feelings?"

이렇게도 표현할 수 있어요!

(Why don't we - ?)
Let's talk it out.
Let's have a talk.
Let's talk about it.
Let's share our feelings.
Let's discuss what happened.
Let's talk about what happened.

서로 안아주고 같이 이야기해보자

시온맘's Pick

"Let's hug one another and share our feelings."

다양하게 표현할 수 있어요!

Let's hug. + *
Let's hug each other. + *
Let's hug one another. + *
Let's give each other a hug. + *

* and talk it out.
* and have a talk.
* and talk about it.
* and share our feelings.
* and discuss what happened.
* and talk about what happened.

Let's hug and talk together.

시온맘's Pick

"Why don't we **hug one another** and share our feelings?"

이렇게도 표현할 수 있어요!

(Why don't we - ?)

Let's hug. + *
Let's hug each other. + *
Let's hug one another. + *
Let's give each other a hug. + *

* and talk it out.
* and have a talk.
* and talk about it.
* and share our feelings.
* and discuss what happened.
* and talk about what happened.

우리 애기 / 아들 / 딸 안으니까 기분 좋네

시온맘's Pick

"It makes me happy to have you in my arms."

다양하게 표현할 수 있어요!

It feels so good to hug you.
great

It feels so good hugging you.
great

Hugging you makes me feel better.

It makes me happy to have you in my arms.

It's such a great feeling to have you in my arms.

엄마는 너를 품에 안는 게 참 좋더라

시온맘's Pick

"I love cuddling you."

다양하게 표현할 수 있어요!

I love hugging you.
I love cuddling (with) you.
I love having you in my arms.
There's no one else I'd rather hug.
Nothing can compare to hugging you.
Hugging you always makes me feel good.

앉히기

Making Them Sit

이리 와서 앉아보렴

시온맘's Pick

"Come this way and have a seat over here."

다양하게 표현할 수 있어요!

(+ Please)
Sit here.
Be seated.
Sit over here.
Sit down here.
Come sit over here.
Grab a seat over here.
Have a seat over here.
Come over here and have a seat.

(+ Please)
Come this way (and) sit here.
be seated.
sit over here.
sit down here.
grab a seat over here.
have a seat over here.

시온맘's Pick

"Won't you come this way and have a seat over here?"

이렇게도 표현할 수 있어요!

(+ Won't you - ?)
(+ Why don't you - ?)

Sit here.
Be seated.
Sit over here.
Sit down here.
Come sit over here.
Grab a seat over here.
Have a seat over here.
Come over here and have a seat.

(+ Won't you - ?)
(+ Why don't you - ?)

Come this way (and) sit here.
be seated.
sit over here.
sit down here.
grab a seat over here.
have a seat over here.

이리 와서 앉아보렴

시온맘's Pick

"Come have a seat in front of me."

다양하게 표현할 수 있어요!

(+ Please)

(엄마 앞에 앉는 경우)

Come (and) sit in front of me.

Come (and) have a seat in front of me.

시온맘's Pick

"Come have a seat beside me."

다양하게 표현할 수 있어요!

(+ Please)

(엄마 옆에 앉는 경우)

Come (and) sit beside me.

Come (and) sit next to me.

Come (and) have a seat beside me.

Come (and) have a seat next to me.

예쁘게 앉아 보렴
똑바로 앉아 보렴

시온맘's Pick

"Please have a seat, properly."

★ 다양하게 표현할 수 있어요!

(+ Please)

Sit up straight.
Sit (down) nicely.
Sit in a nice posture.
Sit (down) properly.

(+ Please)

Have a seat, nicely.
properly.

(+ Please 안 됨)

Can you try sitting up straight?
Can you try sitting (down) nicely?
Can you try sitting in a nice posture?
Can you try sitting (down) properly?

장난치지 말고

시온맘's Pick

"Please stop horsing around."

다양하게 표현할 수 있어요!

(+ Please)

Don't goof off.
Don't joke around.
Don't play around.
Don't goof around.
Don't horse around.

(+ Please)

Stop goofing off.
Quit goofing off.

Stop joking around.
Quit joking around.

Stop playing around.
Quit playing around.

Stop goofing around.
Quit goofing around.

Stop horsing around.
Quit horsing around.

* 위 문장들 전이나 후에 "Mommy said" 또는 "I said"를 붙이면 조금 더 단호한 느낌이 날 수 있습니다.
* Goof off : 빈둥거리다
  (할 일을 안 하고 시간을 낭비하는 뉘앙스)
* Horse around : 법석을 떨다
  (말처럼 법석을 떨며 장난치는 뉘앙스)

얌전히 앉아 있어보자

시온맘's Pick

"Stay in your seat."

다양하게 표현할 수 있어요!

(+ Please)
Sit still.
Stay still.
Stay seated.
Remain seated.
Stay in your seat.

시온맘's Pick

"Try to stay in your seat."

이렇게도 표현할 수 있어요!

(+ Try to -)
Sit still.
Stay still.
Stay seated.
Remain seated.
Stay in your seat.

도망가지 말고 여기 가만히 있으렴

시온맘's Pick

"Stay put here."

다양하게 표현할 수 있어요!

(+ Please)
Stay put here.
Stay right here.
Don't run away from me.
Don't you walk away from me.
Don't walk away and stay right here.

눈높이 맞추기

Matching Their Eye Level

고개 들어보렴

시온맘's Pick

"Please put your face up."

다양하게 표현할 수 있어요!

(+ Please 안 됨)

Face up!

(+ Please)

Look up.
Lift your chin.
Put your face up.
Lift your head up.
Keep your head up.

엄마 봐봐

시온맘's Pick

"Look at mommy in the eyes."

다양하게 표현할 수 있어요!

Look this way.

Look into my eyes.

Look at me.
mommy.

Eyes on me.
mommy.

Keep your eyes on me.
mommy.

Look at me in the eyes.
mommy

* 엄마가 아이에게 자신을 표현하는 경우, 문장의 목적어로 Me와 Mom보다는 Mommy를 더 많이 사용합니다. 더 친근한 느낌을 담고 있기 때문입니다.

다른 데 보지 말고,
엄마랑 눈 좀 마주칠 수 있니

시온맘's Pick

"Don't look that way."

다양하게 표현할 수 있어요!

Don't look away.
Stop looking away.
Don't look that way.
Stop looking at the other direction.

* 위 문장들 전이나 후에 아래 표현들 중 하나를 더할 수 있습니다.

* I'm right here.
* I'm right over here.

시온맘's Pick

"I'm right over here. Don't look that way."

시온맘's Pick

"Could you give mommy your attention?"

이렇게도 표현할 수 있어요!

(Could you - ?)

Can you look at me in the eyes?
mommy

Can you give me your attention?
mommy

Can you pay attention to me?
mommy?

Don't look elsewhere. Keep your eyes on me.
mommy.

Don't look the other way and look at me in the eyes.
mommy

* 엄마가 아이에게 자신을 표현하는 경우, 문장의 목적어로 Me와 Mom보다는 Mommy를 더 많이 사용합니다. 더 친근한 느낌을 담고 있기 때문입니다.

엄마 얼굴 보면서 이야기 나누자

시온맘's Pick

"Look mommy in the eyes, let's talk."

다양하게 표현할 수 있어요!

Look into my eyes, let's talk.
have a talk.

Look at me, let's talk.
mommy,

Look at me, let's have a talk.
mommy,

Eyes on me, let's talk.
mommy,

Eyes on me, let's have a talk.
mommy,

Look me in the eyes, let's talk.
mommy

Look me in the eyes, let's have a talk.
mommy

* 엄마가 아이에게 자신을 표현하는 경우, 문장의 목적어로 Me와 Mom보다는 Mommy를 더 많이 사용합니다. 더 친근한 느낌을 담고 있기 때문입니다.

마음 달래기

ComfortingaChild

감정 달래기

Comforting Them

울지 마. 괜찮아

시온맘's Pick

"There's no need to cry. It's going to be all right."

다양하게 표현할 수 있어요!

Don't cry. + *
You don't have to cry. + *
You don't need to cry. + *
There's no need to cry. + *
Stop crying and calm down. + *
There's no need for you to cry. + *
There's no reason for you to cry. + *

* It's all right.
* It's (all) okay.
* Everything is okay.
* Everything's all right.
* It's going to be okay.
* It's going to be all right.

(아이 기분이 안 좋은 경우)

마음 가라 앉히고 진정해, 괜찮아

시온맘's Pick

"Simmer down. Everything is all right."

다양하게 표현할 수 있어요!

Relax. + *
Get calm. + *
Loosen up. + *
Calm down. + *
Take it easy. + *
Settle down. + *
Calm yourself. + *
Simmer down. + *
Control yourself. + *
Pull yourself together. + *
Get a hold of yourself. + *

* It's all right.
* It's (all) okay.
* Everything is okay.
* Everything's all right.
* It's going to be okay.
* It's going to be all right.

* 위 문장들 전이나 후에 다음 아래 표현들 중 하나를 더할 수 있습니다.

* Don't worry.
* You don't have to worry.
* There's no need for you to worry.

시온맘's Pick

"Simmer down. Everything is all right. Don't worry."

엄마 화내는 거 아니야, 울지 마렴

시온맘's Pick

"Mommy is not mad at you. You shouldn't cry."

다양하게 표현할 수 있어요!

Don't worry. + *

I'm not mad at you. + *
angry at you. + *
upset with you. + *

Mommy is not mad at you. + *
angry at you. + *
upset with you. + *

* You shouldn't cry.
* You can stop crying.
* Can you stop crying?
* Could you stop crying?

* 엄마가 아이에게 자신을 표현하는 경우, 문장의 주어로 I와 Mom보다는 Mommy를 더 많이 사용합니다. 더 친근한 느낌을 담고 있기 때문입니다.

눈물 멈추고 짜증 내지 않고 이야기해주면 엄마가 네 이야기를 더 잘 이해할 수 있단다

시온맘's Pick

"I need you to stop throwing a fit and talk to me. That way, I can understand you better."

다양하게 표현할 수 있어요!

I can't understand you unless you stop crying.
throwing a fit.

If you are not mad at me, I can understand you better.
I'll be able to

If you are not upset with me, I can understand you better.
I'll be able to

Unless you stop crying and talk to me, I can't understand you.

If you stop crying and talk to me, I can understand you better.
am able to

I need you to stop crying so I can understand you better.

I need you to stop crying and talk to me. That way, I can
throwing a fit
understand you better.

Once you stop throwing a fit, I can understand you better.
will be able to

Once you stop crying and are no longer mad at me,
I can understand you better.
will be able to

너무 속상해마렴

시온맘's Pick

"Don't let it get to you."

★ 다양하게 표현할 수 있어요!

Don't let it get to you.
Don't be (so / too) sad.
Don't feel (so / too) bad.
Don't be (so / too) upset.
Don't take it (so / too) hard.

* 상황에 따라 feel bad는 "죄책감 갖지 마", "너무 미안해 하지 마" 등의 의미로 사용되기도 합니다.

* Don't be (so / too) upset.

* 다음 문장에서 부사 so 또는 too를 생략하지 않았을 때, 두 개의 부사 중 하나에 강세를 두고 발음할 경우, "그렇게 화내지 마" 의미로 전달되기도 합니다.

시온맘's Pick

"You shouldn't be so upset."

★ 이렇게도 표현할 수 있어요!

You shouldn't be (so / too) sad.
You shouldn't feel (so / too) bad.

You shouldn't be (so / too) upset.
You shouldn't take it (so / too) hard.

시온맘's Pick

"There's no need for you to be upset."

이렇게도 표현할 수 있어요!

I don't want you to feel sad.
bad.
upset.

There's no need for you to be sad.
upset.

There's no need for you to feel sad.
bad.
upset.

* 정리된 전체 문장들 전이나 후에 아래 표현들 중 하나를 더할 수 있습니다.

* Loosen up.
* Take it easy.

시온맘's Pick

"Loosen up. Don't let it get to you."

이제 진정됐니?

시온맘's Pick

"Have you calmed down?"

다양하게 표현할 수 있어요!

Are you okay now?
How do you feel now?
Have you calmed down?
Do you feel better (now)?
Are you feeling better (now)?
Are you ready to talk to me (now)?

* Are you ready to talk to me (now)?

엄마와 이야기를 나눌 수 있는 마음 상태인지 확인하고 달래는 뉘앙스를 담고 있습니다.

아직도 울고 있네

시온맘's Pick

"I see tears, still."

다양하게 표현할 수 있어요!

I see tears, still.
You're still crying.
You haven't stopped crying yet.

괜찮아, 울어도 돼

시온맘's Pick

"You don't have to hold it."

다양하게 표현할 수 있어요!

You can cry.
It's okay (for you) to cry.
You don't have to hold it (in).
You can cry until you feel better.
You don't need to hold in your tears.
It's all right. You can cry if that makes you feel better.

울면서 마음 가라앉혀볼까

시온맘's Pick

"Why don't you try to calm yourself through crying?"

다양하게 표현할 수 있어요!

Why don't you try to calm yourself by crying?
through

울면서 마음 잘 가라앉혀보자

시온맘's Pick

"Cry as much as you want and see if it makes you feel better."

다양하게 표현할 수 있어요!

You should try to calm yourself by crying.
through

Cry as much as you want and see if it makes you feel better.

상황 이해하기

Understanding Their Behavior

그것 때문에 많이 놀랐니?

시온맘's Pick

"Were you frightened by that?"

다양하게 표현할 수 있어요!

* 전체 문장에서 it과 this는 모두 that으로 대신 표현할 수 있습니다.

Did it scare you?
surprise
frighten

Did it make you scared?
surprised?
frightened?

Did it make you feel scared?

Were you scared by it?
surprised
frightened

Is this what scared you?
surprised
frightened

Is this what made you scared?
surprised?
frightened?

* 이어지는 아래 표현들은 아이의 마음을 더 깊이 공감해주는 느낌을 담고 있습니다.

시온맘's Pick

"You must've been frightened by that. Am I right?"

이렇게도 표현할 수 있어요!

You must've been scared by it. + *
frightened

* Right?
* Am I right?
* Is that right?

그래서 울었구나
놀라서 울었구나

시온맘's Pick

"I see why you cried."

다양하게 표현할 수 있어요!

It made you cry.
That

I see why you cried.
That's

You cried because of it.
that.

That's what made you cry.

You were scared, so you cried.
startled
surprised
frightened

You cried because you were scared.
startled.
surprised.
frightened.

* 위 문장들 전이나 후에 다음 표현을 더할 수 있습니다.

* I understand now.

시온맘's Pick

"I see why you cried. I understand now."

시온맘's Pick

"Now I see why you cried."

이렇게도 표현할 수 있어요!

Now I see why you cried.
understand

(아이가 숨차게 울고 있을 경우)

크게 숨을 쉬어 보자, 좀 나아질 거야

시온맘's Pick

"Take a deep breath, then breathe out. It will be much better."

다양하게 표현할 수 있어요!

(Slowly) Breathe in. + *
(Slowly) Breathe in, breathe out. + *
Take a deep breath, then breathe out. + *

* You'll be better.
* You'll feel better.
* It will be much better.
* It'll make you feel better.
* It'll make you feel a lot better.

엄마가 네 마음을 몰라줘서 속상했구나

시온맘's Pick

"You felt upset as I didn't read your mind."

다양하게 표현할 수 있어요!

You felt sad as I didn't read you.
bad — read your mind.
upset

You felt sad as I didn't hear you (out).
bad
upset

You were sad as I didn't understand you.
upset

You were sad as I didn't know how you felt.
upset

* as 자리에 대체 가능한 접속사들입니다. * for * because

시온맘's Pick

"You felt upset for I didn't read your mind."

시온맘's Pick

"You felt that I didn't hear you, so you were upset."

이렇게도 표현할 수 있어요!

You felt that I didn't understand you, so you were sad.
upset.

You felt that I didn't hear you (out), so you were sad.
upset.

무슨 말인지 알겠구나
엄마가 네 마음을 이해한단다
네 기분이 어떤지 엄마가 잘 알아

시온맘's Pick

"I quite get you."

다양하게 표현할 수 있어요!

I feel you.
hear

I get you completely.
understand

I (fully / quite) get you.
understand

I see what you mean.
get
know
understand

I see what you are saying.
get
know
understand

I see your point.
get
understand

I get how you feel.
know
understand

I see what you are trying to say.
get
know
understand

I see things from your point of view.

* 문장들 끝에 자녀를 부를 때 사용하는 애칭을 붙여주셔도 좋습니다.

* Love
* Dear
* Lovely
* Honey
* Sweetie

시온맘's Pick

"I quite get you, Sweetie."

* 자녀의 마음을 더 깊이 공감하는 느낌으로 소통하기 원하실 경우,
문장 끝에 "I do"를 더할 수 있습니다.

시온맘's Pick

"I quite get you, Sweetie. I do."

놀랐겠구나

시온맘's Pick

"You've been startled."

다양하게 표현할 수 있어요!

You've been scared.
startled.
surprised.
frightened.

You must've been scared.
startled.
surprised.
frightened.

좋은 의도로 그런 거구나

시온맘's Pick

"You were well intentioned."

다양하게 표현할 수 있어요!

It had good intentions.
You had good intentions.
You were well intentioned.
You did it with good intentions.
You did it for a (good) reason.

엄마를 도와주려고 그랬구나

시온맘's Pick

"You were going to help mommy."

다양하게 표현할 수 있어요!

You tried to help me.
mommy.

You were going to help me.
mommy.

You were trying to help me.
mommy.

You just wanted to help me.
mommy.

You were just trying to help me.
mommy.

* 엄마가 아이에게 자신을 표현하는 경우, 문장의 목적어로 Me와 Mom보다는 Mommy를 더 많이 사용합니다. 더 친근한 느낌을 담고 있기 때문입니다.

엄마를 기쁘게 해주려고 그랬구나

시온맘's Pick

"You were going to make mommy happy."

다양하게 표현할 수 있어요!

You tried to make me happy.
mommy

You were trying to make me happy.
mommy

You were going to make me happy.
mommy

You just wanted to make me happy.
mommy

You were just trying to make me happy.
mommy

* 엄마가 아이에게 자신을 표현하는 경우, 문장의 목적어로 Me와 Mom보다는 Mommy를 더 많이 사용합니다. 더 친근한 느낌을 담고 있기 때문입니다.

엄마가 일부러 그런 건 아니란다

시온맘's Pick

"That is not what I meant."

다양하게 표현할 수 있어요!

* 전체 문장에서 it은 모두 that으로 대신 표현할 수 있습니다.

I didn't mean it.
I didn't mean to.
I didn't mean to do it.

It was an accident.
It was not intentional.

I didn't do it on purpose.

It is not what I meant.
It is not what I meant to do.

엄마도 이렇게 될 줄 몰랐어

시온맘's Pick

"I didn't mean for it to happen."

다양하게 표현할 수 있어요!

I didn't mean for it to happen.
I didn't want it to happen that way.

엄마가 미안해, 그만 화 풀어

시온맘's Pick

"I'm sorry. Don't stay angry at me."

다양하게 표현할 수 있어요!

I'm sorry. I want you to feel better.

I'm sorry. (Please) Don't stay mad at me.
angry

I'm sorry. (Please) Stop being mad at me.

I want to say sorry to you. Could you tell me it's okay?

엄마가 오해해서 미안해

시온맘's Pick

"Sorry, I got you wrong."

다양하게 표현할 수 있어요!

Sorry, I was wrong.
Sorry, I didn't know.
Sorry, I got you wrong.
Sorry, I misunderstood you.
Sorry, I was mistaken about you.
Sorry about the misunderstanding.

기분 나쁘게 해서 미안해

시온맘's Pick

"Sorry that I hurt your feelings."

다양하게 표현할 수 있어요!

Sorry to offend you.

Sorry that I hurt you.
your feelings.

Sorry that I made you feel bad.

Sorry for making you feel that way.

미안해, 기분 나쁘게 하려던 건 아니었어

시온맘's Pick

"Sorry, I didn't intend on making you feel bad."

다양하게 표현할 수 있어요!

Sorry, I didn't mean to offend you.

Sorry, I didn't mean to make you feel sad.
bad.
upset.

Sorry, I wasn't trying to make you feel sad.
bad.
upset.

Sorry, I didn't intend on making you feel sad.
bad.
upset.

Sorry, it wasn't my intention to make you feel sad.
bad.
upset.

* Sorry 자리를 대신할 수 있는 표현들입니다. * I'm sorry. * I apologize.

시온맘's Pick

"I apologize. I didn't intend on making you feel bad."

엄마가 장난(농담)한 거야

시온맘's Pick

"I was just joking around."

다양하게 표현할 수 있어요!

* 전체 문장에서 it은 모두 that으로 대신 표현할 수 있습니다.

I was joking.
kidding.

It was a joke.
That

It's just a joke.
That's

I was just joking (around).

I didn't mean it. I was only joking.
kidding.

(그 말을 들으니) 안됐네

시온맘's Pick

I'm sorry to hear that.

그래서 속상했구나

시온맘's Pick

"So you were mad."

다양하게 표현할 수 있어요!

So you felt sad.
bad.
upset.

So you were sad.
mad.
upset.

* So 자리를 That's why 로 대신할 수 있습니다.

시온맘's Pick

"That's why you were mad."

실수했었구나

시온맘's Pick

"You did that by accident."

다양하게 표현할 수 있어요!

* 전체 문장에서 it은 모두 that으로 대신 표현할 수 있습니다.

It was a mistake.
an accident.

You did it by mistake.
accident.

You made a mistake.

You didn't mean to do it.

* 자녀의 마음을 더 깊이 공감하는 느낌으로 소통하기 원하실 경우, 위 문장들 전이나 후에 "I see"를 더해주셔도 좋습니다.

시온맘's Pick

"You did that by accident. I see."

시온맘's Pick

"I know you made a mistake."

이렇게도 표현할 수 있어요!

I (now) know you made a mistake.

뜻대로 안돼서 속상했구나

시온맘's Pick

"You were sad because it didn't go as you planned."

다양하게 표현할 수 있어요!

You were sad because it didn't work out.
mad
upset

You were sad because you couldn't do it.
mad
upset

You were sad because it didn't go as you planned.
mad
upset

You were sad because it didn't work (out) the way you wanted.
mad
upset

* because 자리에 대체 가능한 접속사들입니다.

* as * for

시온맘's Pick

"You were sad as it didn't go as you planned."

다독이기

Consoling Them

괜찮을 거야

시온맘's Pick

"You are going to be okay."

다양하게 표현할 수 있어요!

Everything will be fine.
okay.
all right.

You are going to be fine.
okay.
all right.

토닥토닥

시온맘's Pick

"There. There."

엄마 여기 있어

시온맘's Pick

"Mommy is right next to you."

다양하게 표현할 수 있어요!

I'm (right) here.
(right) next to you.
not going anywhere.

Mommy is (right) here.
(right) next to you.
not going anywhere.

* 엄마가 아이에게 자신을 표현하는 경우, 문장의 주어로 I와 Mom보다는 Mommy를 더 많이 사용합니다. 더 친근한 느낌을 담고 있기 때문입니다.

너무 두려워하지 않아도 돼, 엄마 여기 있단다

시온맘's Pick

"Don't be afraid. Mommy is right next to you."

다양하게 표현할 수 있어요!

Don't worry. + *
be afraid. + *

You don't have to worry. + *
be afraid. + *

* I'm (right) here.
(right) next to you.
not going anywhere.

* Mommy is (right) here.
(right) next to you.
not going anywhere.

* 엄마가 아이에게 자신을 표현하는 경우, 문장의 주어로 I와 Mom보다는 Mommy를 더 많이 사용합니다. 더 친근한 느낌을 담고 있기 때문입니다.

기분이 안 좋아 보이네

시온맘's Pick

"You look down."

다양하게 표현할 수 있어요!

You look blue.
down.
depressed.
very upset.

You seem blue.
down.
depressed.
very upset.
to be down.

You don't look so satisfied.
seem

You seem to be in a bad mood.

You look like you're in a bad mood.
seem

엄마 따라해보렴

시온맘's Pick

"Try to follow after mommy."

다양하게 표현할 수 있어요!

(+ Please)

Do as I say.
mommy says.

Follow after me.
mommy.

Try to copy me.
mommy.

Try to follow after me.
mommy.

* 엄마가 아이에게 자신을 표현하는 경우, 문장의 주어 또는 목적어로 I, Me, Mom보다는 Mommy를 더 많이 사용합니다. 더 친근한 느낌을 담고 있기 때문입니다.

시온맘's Pick

"Why don't you try to follow after mommy?"

이렇게도 표현할 수 있어요!

(+ Why don't you - ?)

Do as I say.
mommy says.

Follow after me.
mommy.

Try to copy me.
mommy.

Try to follow after me.
mommy.

스스로 너무 자책하지 마렴

시온맘's Pick

"It's not a big problem."

다양하게 표현할 수 있어요!

It's not your fault.
It wasn't your fault.
It's not a big problem.

시온맘's Pick

"Don't be so hard on yourself."

이렇게도 표현할 수 있어요!

Don't blame yourself.
Don't be so hard on yourself.
Don't take it too hard on yourself.

시온맘's Pick

"Try not to be so hard on yourself."

이렇게도 표현할 수 있어요!

(Try not to -)
(You shouldn't -)
Don't blame yourself.
Don't be so hard on yourself.
Don't take it too hard on yourself.

* 정리된 전체 문장들 전이나 후에 아래 표현을 더할 수 있습니다.

* Take it easy.

시온맘's Pick

"You shouldn't be so hard on yourself. Take it easy."

별 거 아냐

시온맘's Pick

"No biggy."

다양하게 표현할 수 있어요!

No biggy.
It's no biggy.

No biggie.
It's no biggie.

* 자녀에게 모두 사용 가능한 Slang입니다.
* Slang : 가까운 관계에서 사용 가능한 은어
* Biggy = Biggie : 구어체로, 중요하고 소중한 것을 의미(앞에 No가 사용되어 별일 아니야! 걱정 마!라는 뉘앙스로 사용됩니다.)

괜찮아, 다음에 더 잘하면 돼

시온맘's Pick

"There's always next time."

다양하게 표현할 수 있어요!

Better luck next time.
There's always next time.
You'll have other chances.
You'll be better next time.
You can do better next time.
You can try again another time.

* 위 문장들 전이나 후에 아래 표현들 중 하나를 더할 수 있습니다. 다만 후보다 전에 표현해주시는 것이 더 자연스럽습니다.

* It's okay.
* It's all right.

시온맘's Pick

"It's all right. There's always next time."

다음에는 더 잘할 거야
엄마는 네가 다음엔 더 잘할 거라 믿어

시온맘's Pick

"I'm sure that next time will be better."

다양하게 표현할 수 있어요!

I'm sure you'll be better next time.

I'm sure you will do better next time.
can

I'm sure that next time will be better.

* 위 문장들 전이나 후에 아래 표현들 중 하나를 더할 수 있습니다.

* I believe in you.
* I have faith in you.

시온맘's Pick

"I'm sure that next time will be better. I believe in you."

격려하기

Encouraging Them

점점 더 잘하고 있어

시온맘's Pick

"You're showing improvement."

다양하게 표현할 수 있어요!

You're improving. + *

I'm seeing progress. + *
improvement. + *

You're showing progress. + *
improvement. + *

You're getting so good at it.
better and better.

You're doing a lot better than before.

I see that you're getting better at this. + *

* 표시된 문장들 뒤에 아래 표현들 중 하나를 더해주셔도 됩니다.

* each day * every day * day by day

시온맘's Pick

"You're showing improvement each day."

좋은 시도였어

시온맘's Pick

"Your effort counts."

다양하게 표현할 수 있어요!

* 밑줄 친 it은 모두 that으로 대신 표현할 수 있습니다.

Your effort counts.

It was a good attempt.

It was a (very) nice try.
good

It's the effort that counts.

You tried and that's what matters.

잘하는 것보다 최선을 다하는 것이 더 중요하단다

시온맘's Pick

Doing your best is more important than being the best.

기운차리고 다시 해보렴

시온맘's Pick

"Keep your pecker up and try it again."

다양하게 표현할 수 있어요!

Cheer up and try it again.

Keep your chin up and try it again.
pecker

그렇게 어렵지 않단다

시온맘's Pick

"It's not that hard."

다양하게 표현할 수 있어요!

It's not too hard.
difficult.

It's not that hard.
difficult.

생각보다 어렵지 않아
보기보다 어렵지 않아

시온맘's Pick

"It's not as difficult as it seems."

다양하게 표현할 수 있어요!

It's not as hard as it looks.
seems.

It's not as difficult as it looks.
seems.

It's not as hard as you think.
difficult

여태까지 잘 해왔어
그동안 잘해왔잖니

시온맘's Pick

"You've done a wonderful job so far."

다양하게 표현할 수 있어요!

You've made it this far.

You've done quite well so far.

You did a good job until now.
great
wonderful

You've done a good job so far.
great
wonderful

You've been doing good (so far).
great
very well

You've been doing a good job (so far).
great
wonderful

처음엔 다 그런 거란다

시온맘's Pick

"We all started that way."

다양하게 표현할 수 있어요!

We all started that way.
The first time is always tough.
There's a first time for everything.
You can't be perfect on your first try
This is only your first time, so it's okay.

네가 최선을 다한 걸 엄마는 알아

시온맘's Pick

"I know you did your utmost."

다양하게 표현할 수 있어요!

I know you did your best.
your utmost.

I know you tried your best.

I know you gave it your best shot.

열심히 노력하는 것 같더라

시온맘's Pick

"I could see that you worked hard."

다양하게 표현할 수 있어요!

I noticed you tried (very) hard.
could see that

I noticed you worked (very) hard.
could see that

You seem to have tried quite a lot.

You seem to have worked (very) hard.

포기하지 않아서 기특해

시온맘's Pick

"I'm proud of you for not giving up."

다양하게 표현할 수 있어요!

I'm impressed you did not give up.
I am glad that you did not give up.
I'm proud of you for not giving up.

실수하면서 배우는 거야

시온맘's Pick

"Your mistakes can help you grow."

다양하게 표현할 수 있어요!

You learn from your mistakes.
Your mistakes can help you grow.

다시 해보는 게 어때

시온맘's Pick

"Why don't you give it another try?"

다양하게 표현할 수 있어요!

Why don't you try again?
Why don't you give it another try?

다시 해보렴
다시 하면 돼

시온맘's Pick

"You can do it over again."

다양하게 표현할 수 있어요!

You can just do it over.
You can (always) try again.
You (always) have more chances.
You can (always) do it (over) again.

잘하고 있어

시온맘's Pick

"You're doing excellent."

다양하게 표현할 수 있어요!

You're doing well.
it well.
very well.

You're doing fine.
good.
great.
excellent.

Keep up the good work.
great

You're coming along (well).

You're doing a good job.
a great job.
a wonderful job.
an excellent job.

지금 훨씬 더 잘하고 있어

시온맘's Pick

"You are doing a lot better."

다양하게 표현할 수 있어요!

You're becoming a pro at this.
You are doing a lot better (than before).
You are doing so much better (than before).

더할 나위 없이 좋아

시온맘's Pick

"It couldn't be any better than this."

다양하게 표현할 수 있어요!

It can't be (any) better.
couldn't

It can't be (any) better than this.
couldn't

여기서 포기하지 마렴

시온맘's Pick

"Don't give up here."

다양하게 표현할 수 있어요!

(+ Please)
Don't give up (now / here).

* 위 문장들 전이나 후에 아래 표현을 더할 수 있습니다.

* You are almost there.

시온맘's Pick

"Please don't give up here. You are almost there."

실망하지 마렴

시온맘's Pick

"Don't be disappointed."

다양하게 표현할 수 있어요!

Don't be so down.

Don't be discouraged.
disappointed.

연습하면 좋아질 거야

시온맘's Pick

"You'll make progress through practice."

다양하게 표현할 수 있어요!

Practice makes perfect.

You'll improve through practice.
do better
get better
make progress

You'll improve by practicing more.
do better
get better
make progress

You'll improve after more practice.
do better
get better
make progress

If you practice more, you will improve.
get better.

The more you practice, the better you'll get at this.
that.

시도해줘서 고맙구나

시온맘's Pick

"Thanks for giving it a shot."

다양하게 표현할 수 있어요!

Thanks for trying.

Thanks for giving it a try.
a shot

* Thanks 자리를 대신할 수 있는 표현입니다.

* Thank you

시온맘's Pick

"Thank you for giving it a shot."

노력해줘서 고맙구나

시온맘's Pick

"Thanks for your effort."

다양하게 표현할 수 있어요!

Thanks for trying.
your effort.
your hard work.

* Thanks 자리를 대신할 수 있는 표현입니다.

* Thank you

시온맘's Pick

"Thank you for your effort."

다 컸네
언제 이렇게 큰 거야
더 이상 애기가 아니네

시온맘's Pick

"You're not a baby anymore."

다양하게 표현할 수 있어요!

* 딸인 경우 Girl, 아들인 경우 Boy.

You're a big girl now.
You're a big boy now.

You are (all) grown up.
You're not a baby anymore.

시온맘's Pick

"You're not a baby anymore. When did you grow up so much?"

이렇게도 표현할 수 있어요!

You're a big girl now. + *
You're a big boy now. + *

* When did you get so big?

You are (all) grown up. + *
You're not a baby anymore. + *

* When did you grow up so big? / much?

* When did you become such a big girl? / boy?

시간 참 빠르다

시온맘's Pick

"My, how time flies."

다양하게 표현할 수 있어요!

Time flies quick.
so fast.

Time (really / just) flies.

Time passes (by) so fast.
quick.

(Oh, / My,) how time files.

계속 해보는 게 어때

시온맘's Pick

"Let's work on it."

다양하게 표현할 수 있어요!

Let's go on.

Let's keep trying.
going.
working on it.

Let's keep up the good work.
carry

Let's (continue to) work on it.

시온맘's Pick

"Why don't you work on it?"

이렇게도 표현할 수 있어요!

(Why don't you - ?)
Let's go on.

Let's keep trying.
going.
working on it.

Let's keep up the good work.
carry

Let's (continue to) work on it.

걱정마, 금방 괜찮아질 거야

시온맘's Pick

"Don't worry. It's going to be all right soon."

다양하게 표현할 수 있어요!

* Don't worry.

* + It will get better.

* + It will be fine.
  okay.
  all right.

* + It's going to be fine. (soon).
  okay.
  all right.

엄마는 항상 네 편이야

시온맘's Pick

"I'll always be on your side."

다양하게 표현할 수 있어요!

I'm here for you.
I'm in your corner.
I'm always on your side.
I'm behind you all the way.

I'll always have your back.

I'll always be there.
on your side.

I've always been on your side.

같은 뜻과 뉘앙스를 가지고 있는 Slang 표현

I got you.
I've got your back.

* 자녀에게 모두 사용 가능한 Slang입니다.
* Slang : 가까운 관계에서 사용 가능한 은어

상황 들어주기
Hearing Them Out

무슨 일이야?

시온맘's Pick

"Anything wrong?"

다양하게 표현할 수 있어요!

What's wrong?
going on?

Anything wrong?

Is something wrong?

Is everything okay?
all right?

What's the matter?
problem?

Is there a problem?
anything wrong?
something wrong?

* 아래 두 표현은 you에 강세를 두고 발음하셔야 의미 전달이 됩니다.
wrong이나 matter에 강세를 두고 발음하실 경우, "너 왜 그러니?" 의미로 전달되어 뜻이 달라집니다.

* What's wrong with you?
* What's the matter with you?

왜 울고 있니?

시온맘's Pick

"What made you cry?"

다양하게 표현할 수 있어요!

Why are you crying?
What made you cry?

무슨 일 있었니?

시온맘's Pick

"Did something happen?"

다양하게 표현할 수 있어요!

What happened?

Can you tell me what happened?

Did anything happen?
something

엄마한테 이야기해주겠니?

시온맘's Pick

"Could you tell mommy?"

다양하게 표현할 수 있어요!

Can you tell me?
mommy?

Could you tell me?
mommy?

Do you want to tell me?
mommy?

Do you want to talk about it?

* 엄마가 아이에게 자신을 표현하는 경우, 문장의 목적어로 Me 또는 Mom보다는 Mommy를 더 많이 사용합니다. 더 친근한 느낌을 담고 있기 때문입니다.

어디 아프니?

시온맘's Pick

"Are you unwell?"

다양하게 표현할 수 있어요!

Are you sick?
okay?
unwell?
all right?

Are you feeling sick?

Is something bothering you?

어디 다쳤니?

시온맘's Pick

"Did you bump into something?"

다양하게 표현할 수 있어요!

Are you hurt?
Did you get hurt?
Did you get a boo-boo?
Did something hurt you?
Did you bump into something?

시온맘's Pick

"What happened? Did you bump into something?"

이렇게도 표현할 수 있어요!

(+ What happened?)
Are you hurt?
Did you get hurt?
Did you get a boo-boo?
Did something hurt you?
Did you bump into something?

화났니?

시온맘's Pick

"Are you upset?"

다양하게 표현할 수 있어요!

Are you mad?
upset?

Are you in a bad mood?

엄마한테 화났니?

시온맘's Pick

"Are you upset with me?"

다양하게 표현할 수 있어요!

Are you mad at me?
upset with

Did I make you feel sad?
mad?
upset?

뭐 때문에 심술난 거야?
뭐 때문에 이렇게 화가 났니?

시온맘's Pick

"What got you this grumpy?"

다양하게 표현할 수 있어요!

Why are you mad?
angry?
upset?
grumpy?

What made you mad?
angry?
upset?
grumpy?

What got you (this) mad?
angry?
upset?
grumpy?

How come you are so mad?
angry?
upset?
grumpy?

우리 아가 왜 기분이 안 좋을까

시온맘's Pick

"I wonder what got you so grumpy."

다양하게 표현할 수 있어요!

I wonder what's wrong.

I wonder what made you sad.
mad.
angry.
upset.
grumpy.

I wonder what got you so sad.
mad.
angry.
upset.
grumpy.

I want to know why you are sad.
mad.
angry.
upset.
grumpy.

I (really) wonder why you're in a bad mood.

뭐가 그렇게 속상하니?

시온맘's Pick

"What got you so mad?"

다양하게 표현할 수 있어요!

Why are you so sad?
mad?
upset?

What got you so sad?
mad?
upset?

What made you (this) sad?
mad?
upset?

누가 속상하게 했니?

시온맘's Pick

"Did someone make you mad?"

다양하게 표현할 수 있어요!

Who hurt your feelings?

Who made you so sad?
mad?
angry?
upset?

Did someone make you sad?
mad?
angry?
upset?

마음이 불편할 땐,
언제든 엄마에게 이야기해도 좋단다

시온맘's Pick

"If you have something you would like to share, feel free to tell mommy any time you would like."

다양하게 표현할 수 있어요!

You can tell me anything and everything.

If you are feeling down, reach out to mommy.

You can always (come and) talk (to me) about your feelings.
how you feel.
what's on your mind.

You can always (come and) share (with me about) your feelings.
how you feel.
what's on your mind.

If you have something (you want / you would like) to say, feel free to tell mommy any time you want.

If you have something (you want / you would like) to say, feel free to tell mommy any time you would like.

If you have something (you want / you would like) to share, feel free to tell mommy any time you want.

If you have something (you want / you would like) to share, feel free to tell mommy any time you would like.

* 위 문장들 전이나 후에 아래 표현들 중 하나를 더해주셔도 됩니다.

* I'm all ears.

* I'm always here for you.
  open

* I'm always here for you if you need me.
  open

* I'm always here for you when you need me.
  open

시온맘's Pick

"If you have something you would like to share, feel free to tell mommy any time you would like. I'm always open for you if you need me."

엄마는 항상 네 이야기를 들을 준비가 되어 있단다

시온맘's Pick

"I'm always open for you if you want to share anything."

다양하게 표현할 수 있어요!

I'm all ears.

I always want to hear you out.
what you have to say.

I always want to listen to you.
what you have to say.

I'm always ready to hear you out.
what you have to say.

I'm always ready to listen to you.
what you have to say.

I'm always here for you if you want to talk.
share anything.

I'm always open for you if you want to talk.
share anything.

I'm always open to talk to you if you want to talk.
share anything.

교육하기

Teaching Right from Wrong

친구 관계

Interacting with Peers

친구들이랑 놀이터에서 놀자구나

시온맘's Pick

"Let's have some fun at the playground, with your friends."

다양하게 표현할 수 있어요!

Let's play at the playground, with your friends.
Let's have some fun at the playground, with your friends.

시온맘's Pick

"Why don't you have some fun at the playground, with your friends?"

이렇게도 표현할 수 있어요!

(Why don't you -?)
Let's play at the playground, with your friends.
Let's have some fun at the playground, with your friends.

친구도 그네 타고 싶어하네 먼저 타게 해주는 거 어때?

시온맘's Pick

"She wants to play on a swing, too. Why don't you let her go first?"

다양하게 표현할 수 있어요!

* 친구가 남자인 경우 He, Him, 여자인 경우 She, Her.

He wants to ride the swing, too. Why don't you let him go first?
She her

* 상황에 맞게 밑줄 친 자리에 대체할 수 있는 표현들입니다.

* 그네를 타다 : try the swing
get on a swing
play on a swing

* 시소를 타다 : ride a seesaw
try the seesaw
get on a seesaw
play on a seesaw

* 미끄럼틀을 타다 : slide down
try the slide
play on a slide
go down a slide

* 구름사다리를 타다 : try the monkey bars
play on the monkey bars
climb up the monkey bars

* 회전뺑뺑이를 타다 : ride a merry-go-round
try the merry-go-round
get on a merry-go-round

* 철봉에 매달리다 : try the horizontal bar
hang down from a horizontal bar

양보해서 이쁘구나

시온맘's Pick

"It's very nice of you to let him go first."

다양하게 표현할 수 있어요!

* 친구가 남자인 경우 Him, 여자인 경우 Her.

It's (very) nice of you to let him go first.
her

미끄럼틀 한 번 타볼래?

시온맘's Pick

"Do you want to go down a slide?"

다양하게 표현할 수 있어요!

Do you want to try the slide?

시온맘's Pick

"Would you like to go down a slide?"

이렇게도 표현할 수 있어요!

(Would you like - ?)
Do you want to try the slide?

* 상황에 맞게 밑줄 친 자리에 대체할 수 있는 표현들입니다.

* 그네를 타다 : try the swing
get on a swing
play on a swing

* 시소를 타다 : ride a seesaw
try the seesaw
get on a seesaw
play on a seesaw

* 미끄럼틀을 타다 : slide down
try the slide
play on a slide
go down a slide

* 구름사다리를 타다 : try the monkey bars
play on the monkey bars
climb up the monkey bars

* 회전뱅뱅이를 타다 : ride a merry-go-round
try the merry-go-round
get on a merry-go-round

* 철봉에 매달리다 : try the horizontal bar
hang down from a horizontal bar

엄마가 여기 있을게

시온맘's Pick

"I'll be staying right here."

다양하게 표현할 수 있어요!

I'll stay (right) here.
stand

I'll be staying (right) here.
standing

엄마가 옆에 있을게

시온맘's Pick

"I'll be standing next to you."

다양하게 표현할 수 있어요!

I'll stay next to you.
stand

I'll be staying (right) next to you.
standing

엄마가 여기서 보고 있을게

시온맘's Pick

"I'll keep an eye on you from here."

다양하게 표현할 수 있어요!

I'll watch you from here.

I'll keep an eye on you from here.
my eyes

친구랑 같이 놀까?

시온맘's Pick

"Do you want to hang out with your friend?"

다양하게 표현할 수 있어요!

Do you want to play with your friend?
Do you want to hang out with your friend?
Do you want to spend some time with your friend?

시온맘's Pick

"Should we hang out with your friend?"

이렇게도 표현할 수 있어요!

(Shall we - ?)
(Should we - ?)
Do you want to play with your friend?
Do you want to hang out with your friend?
Do you want to spend some time with your friend?

시온맘's Pick

"Would you want to hang out with your friend?"

이렇게도 표현할 수 있어요!

(Would you like - ?)
(Would you want - ?)
Do you want to play with your friend?
Do you want to hang out with your friend?
Do you want to spend some time with your friend?

친구에게 가서 같이 놀고 싶은지 물어볼래?

시온맘's Pick

"Do you want to walk over to your friend and ask if he wants to play together?"

다양하게 표현할 수 있어요!

* 친구가 남자인 경우 He, 여자인 경우 She.

Do you want to walk over to your friend and ask if he/she wants to play together?

Do you want to go over to your friend and see if he/she wants to play together?

시온맘's Pick

"Why don't you walk over to your friend and ask if he wants to play together?"

이렇게도 표현할 수 있어요!

(Why don't you - ?)

Do you want to walk over to your friend and ask if he/she wants to play together?

Do you want to go over to your friend and see if he/she wants to play together?

(장난감) 친구가 이거 가지고 놀고 싶대?

시온맘's Pick

"Your friend wants to play with this?"

다양하게 표현할 수 있어요!

* 친구가 남자인 경우 He, 여자인 경우 She.

Your friend wants to play with this?

Does your friend want to play with this?

Did your friend say he wants to play with this?
she

(장난감) 같이 가지고 놀면 어떨까?

시온맘's Pick

"Wouldn't it be a good idea to share?"

다양하게 표현할 수 있어요!

How about sharing?

Why don't you share it as you play?
Why don't you take turns and share?
Why don't you play with it together?

Wouldn't it be a good idea to share?

친구들과 같이 가지고 노는 게 좋겠어

시온맘's Pick

"Sharing is a good thing to do between friends."

다양하게 표현할 수 있어요!

You should share with your friends.
Friends should play with the toys together.
Sharing is a good thing to do between friends.

착한 아이는 나눌 줄 안단다

시온맘's Pick

"Sharing makes you a good friend."

다양하게 표현할 수 있어요!

* 친구가 남자인 경우 Boy, 여자인 경우 Girl.

Good girls share.
boys
friends

Sharing makes you a good girl.
boy.
friend.

A good boy knows how to share.
girl
friend

A good boy knows how to play together.
girl
friend

(장난감) 같이 가지고 놀렴

시온맘's Pick

"Be a good friend and play with the toys together."

다양하게 표현할 수 있어요!

Let your friend play with your toys.

You should share the toys with your friend.

You should share your toys for a little while.

Be a good friend and share.
play with the toys together.

같이 가지고 놀자

시온맘's Pick

"Try sharing."

다양하게 표현할 수 있어요!

Share.
Try sharing.
Play together.
Play with it together.
them

시온맘's Pick

"Why don't you try sharing?"

이렇게도 표현할 수 있어요!

(+ Let's -)
(+ Why don't you - ?)
Share.
Try sharing.
Play together.
Play with it together.
them

같이 가지고 놀면 더 재밌단다

시온맘's Pick

"You can play together for more fun."

다양하게 표현할 수 있어요!

You can share for more fun.
play together

Playing together is (a lot) more fun.

Playing together will be (a lot) more fun.
Sharing

It's (a lot) more fun if you share (it).
play together.

집에 장난감 많잖니

시온맘's Pick

"You have plenty of toys at home."

다양하게 표현할 수 있어요!

You have tons of toys at home.
a lot of
plenty of

엄마가 다음에 또 사줄게

시온맘's Pick

"I will buy you one next time."

다양하게 표현할 수 있어요!

I will buy you one (more) next time.
I will buy one (more) for you next time.

양보하는 모습 정말 멋졌어, 엄마 감동했어

시온맘's Pick

"It was very nice of you that you shared with her. That was kind."

다양하게 표현할 수 있어요!

* 친구가 남자인 경우 Him, 여자인 경우 Her.

It was very nice of you to share that. That was kind.

It was very nice of you that you shared with him. That was kind.
her.

It was very nice of you to share that. I was (so) moved.
touched.
impressed.

It was very nice of you that you shared with him. I was (so) moved.
her. touched.
impressed.

말 조심하렴

시온맘's Pick

"Watch your language."

다양하게 표현할 수 있어요!

(+ Please)

Watch it.
your mouth.
your language.

Be careful what you say.

Be careful with your words.

(+ Please 안 됨)

You shouldn't say that.

말 예쁘게 해야지

시온맘's Pick

"You need to speak nicely."

다양하게 표현할 수 있어요!

Say it nicely.

Speak nicely.

You should say it nicely.
need to

You should speak it nicely.
need to

그런 말 하지 마렴, 그건 욕이야

시온맘's Pick

"You shouldn't say that. That's a swearing word."

다양하게 표현할 수 있어요!

Don't say that. + *
That's not nice. + *
You shouldn't say that. + *
That's not a nice word to say. + *

* That's a bad word.
* That's a swearing word.

그렇게 말하면 안 돼

시온맘's Pick

"You shouldn't talk like that."

다양하게 표현할 수 있어요!

You mustn't talk like that.
shouldn't
had better not

You mustn't say it like that.
shouldn't
had better not

You mustn't speak that way.
shouldn't
had better not

그렇게 말하면
- 친구가 서운할 수 있단다
- 친구가 기분 나쁠 수 있단다

시온맘's Pick

"If you talk like that, she may feel upset."

다양하게 표현할 수 있어요!

* 친구가 남자인 경우 He, 여자인 경우 She.

He may feel sad, if you speak that way.
She bad,
Your friend mad,
upset,

If you say it like that, he may feel sad.
talk she bad.
speak mad.
upset.

시온맘's Pick

"If you talk like that, she might be upset."

이렇게도 표현할 수 있어요!

(may be / might be / can be / could be)
(may feel / might feel / can feel / could feel)

He may feel sad, if you speak that way.
She bad,
Your friend mad,
upset,

If you say it like that, he may feel sad.
talk she bad.
speak mad.
pset.

말로 하렴

시온맘's Pick

"You should speak."

다양하게 표현할 수 있어요!

You should speak.
You should use your words.

시온맘's Pick

"You need to speak."

이렇게도 표현할 수 있어요!

(You need to -)
You should speak.
You should use your words.

손 가만히 바로 하렴

시온맘's Pick

"Keep your hands to yourself."

다양하게 표현할 수 있어요!

(+ Please)
Keep your hands to yourself.

발 가만히 바로 하렴

시온맘's Pick

"Keep your feet to yourself."

다양하게 표현할 수 있어요!

(+ Please)
Keep your feet to yourself.

던지면 안 돼
던지는 건 안 돼

시온맘's Pick

"Throwing is not a right thing to do."

다양하게 표현할 수 있어요!

No throwing!

Throwing is not nice.
right.

You should not throw things.

Throwing is not a nice thing to do.
right

* 아래 두 문장은 매우 단호한 표현입니다.

* Throwing is not allowed.
acceptable.

던지는 건 나쁜 행동이란다

시온맘's Pick

"Throwing is bad behavior."

다양하게 표현할 수 있어요!

Throwing is bad.
wrong.
bad behavior.

Throwing is not nice at all.

화난다고 물건을 던지는 건 아니란다

시온맘's Pick

"No matter how angry you are, you must not throw things."

다양하게 표현할 수 있어요!

You must not throw anything even when you are mad.
angry.
upset.

No matter how mad you are, you must not throw things.
angry
upset

친구 때리면 안 돼

시온맘's Pick

"Hitting your friend is not a right thing to do."

다양하게 표현할 수 있어요!

No hitting!

Don't hit your friend.

You'd better not hit your friend.

You mustn't hit your friend (like that).
shouldn't

Hitting (your friend) is not a nice thing to do.
right

* 아래 두 문장은 매우 단호한 표현입니다.

* Hitting is not allowed.
acceptable.

때리는 건 나쁜 행동이야

시온맘's Pick

"Hitting is not right."

다양하게 표현할 수 있어요!

Hitting is bad.

Hitting is not a nice thing to do.
right

Hitting (your friend) is not nice.
right.

친구도 아프단다
때리면 친구가 아프단다

시온맘's Pick

"It could hurt your friend, too."

다양하게 표현할 수 있어요!

* 친구가 남자인 경우 Him, 여자인 경우 Her.

Hitting can hurt others.

Your friend is hurt, too.

It could hurt your friend, too.

Your friend can get hurt if you hit him.
her.

When you hit your friend, it can hurt him.
her.

When you hit your friend, your friend is hurt, too.

맒이 아프지?

시온맘's Pick

"It hurts, doesn't it?"

다양하게 표현할 수 있어요!

Doesn't it hurt?

It hurts (a lot), right?
doesn't it?

이렇게 싸우면 아프겠지?

시온맘's Pick

"Wouldn't it hurt if you hit and fight like this?"

다양하게 표현할 수 있어요!

It hurts when you fight like this, right?
doesn't it?

When you hit and fight, it hurts, right?
doesn't it?

Wouldn't it hurt if you hit and fight like this?

아무리 화가 나도 때리면 안 돼

시온맘's Pick

"No matter how angry you are, hitting is not an acceptable behavior."

다양하게 표현할 수 있어요!

Even if you are mad, you mustn't hit others.
angry, shouldn't
upset,

Don't hit others, no matter how mad you are.
angry
upset

Even when you are mad, hitting is not the best idea.
angry,
upset,

No matter how mad you are, hitting is not an acceptable behavior.
angry
upset

그렇다고 그렇게 하면 안 된단다

시온맘's Pick

"But you had better not behave that way."

다양하게 표현할 수 있어요!

(+ But -)

That doesn't mean you can act like that.
act that way.
behave that way.

That doesn't make it okay for you to act like that.
act that way.
behave that way.

* 조언의 강도 조절 Should not < had better not < must not

(But -)

Even so, you must not act like that.
act that way.
behave that way.

Even so, you should not act like that.
act that way.
behave that way.

Even so, you had better not act like that.
behave that way.
behave that way.

* 구어체에서는 조동사 had better not을 사용할 경우, had를 생략하고 better not만 사용하기도 합니다.

화가 난다고 해서 그렇게 하면 안 된단다

시온맘's Pick

"Even if you are upset, you should not act that way."

다양하게 표현할 수 있어요!

You shouldn't act like that, even if you are mad.
act that way, angry.
behave that way, upset.
do something like that,

Even if you are mad, you should still behave yourself.
angry,
upset,

Even if you are mad, you should not act that way.
angry, behave that way.
upset,

Even if you are mad, you should not act like that.
angry, act that way.
upset, behave that way.

Just because you are mad, it doesn't give you the right to act like that.
angry, act that way.
upset, behave that way.

그런 말하면 부끄러운 거야

시온맘's Pick

"I don't want to hear that."

먼저 뭐라고 해야 하지?

시온맘's Pick

"What should you say first?"

빌려줄 수 있는지 물어봐야지

시온맘's Pick

"Ask if it's okay for you to borrow it."

다양하게 표현할 수 있어요!

* 친구가 남자인 경우 He, Him, 여자인 경우 She, Her.

Go ask him if he can lend it to you.
her she

Ask if it's okay for you to use it.
borrow

You can ask him if you can use.
should her borrow.
play with it.

이건 네 잘못이란다

시온맘's Pick

"This was on you."

다양하게 표현할 수 있어요!

You did this.
This was on you.
This one is on you.
This was your mistake.

이건 친구의 잘못이 아니란다

시온맘's Pick

"It's not her fault."

다양하게 표현할 수 있어요!

* 친구가 남자인 경우 His. 여자인 경우 Her.

It's not his fault.
her

잘못하면 사과하는 거야

시온맘's Pick

"When you do something wrong, you have to say sorry."

다양하게 표현할 수 있어요!

When you make a mistake, you have to say sorry.
do something wrong, apologize.

You have to say sorry when you make a mistake.
do something wrong.

You have to say "I'm Sorry" when you make a mistake.
do something wrong.

시온맘's Pick

"When you do something wrong, you need to say sorry."

이렇게도 표현할 수 있어요!

(- should -)
(- need to -)
(- had better -)

When you make a mistake, you have to say sorry.
do something wrong, apologize.

You have to say sorry when you make a mistake.
do something wrong.

You have to say "I'm Sorry" when you make a mistake.
do something wrong.

화해해보자

시온맘's Pick

"Now let's make up."

미안할 땐 뭐라고 해야 하지?

시온맘's Pick

"What do you say when you are sorry?"

사과해야겠다

시온맘's Pick

"Tell your friend you are sorry."

다양하게 표현할 수 있어요!

Say, "I am sorry."
Apologize to your friend.
Say (that) you are sorry.
Say sorry (to your friend).
Tell your friend (that) you are sorry.

시온맘's Pick

"You should tell your friend that you are sorry."

이렇게도 표현할 수 있어요!

(+ Please)
(+ You should -)
(+ You have to -)
(+ You need to -)
Say, "I am sorry."
Apologize to your friend.
Say (that) you are sorry.
Say sorry (to your friend).
Tell your friend (that) you are sorry.

사과하렴
미안하다고 사과하렴

시온맘's Pick

"Say you are sorry."

다양하게 표현할 수 있어요!

Say, "I am sorry!"
Apologize to your friend.
Say (that) you are sorry.
Say sorry (to your friend).
Tell your friend that you're sorry.

시온맘's Pick

"You should say you are sorry."

이렇게도 표현할 수 있어요!

(+ Please)
(+ You should -)
Say, "I am sorry!"
Apologize to your friend.
Say (that) you are sorry.
Say sorry (to your friend).
Tell your friend that you're sorry.

친구에게 미안하다고 사과해볼래?

시온맘's Pick

"Do you want to apologize to your friend?"

다양하게 표현할 수 있어요!

Do you want to apologize to your friend?
Do you want to say "Sorry" to your friend?
Do you want to tell your friend that you are sorry?

시온맘's Pick

"Can you apologize to you friend?"

이렇게도 표현할 수 있어요!

(Can you - ?)
(Why don't you - ?)
Do you want to apologize to your friend?
Do you want to say "Sorry" to your friend?
Do you want to tell your friend that you are sorry?

미안하다고 하면
친구가 괜찮다고 할 거야

시온맘's Pick

"If you apologize, then your friend will say, 'It's okay'."

다양하게 표현할 수 있어요!

* 친구가 남자인 경우 He, 여자인 경우 She.

If you say sorry, then your friend will say, "It's okay."
apologize,

When you apologize to your friend, he will tell you (that) it's okay.
she

When you tell your friend (that) you are sorry, he will tell you (that) it's okay.
she

그럼 친구 마음이 풀릴 거야

시온맘's Pick

"That will make her feel much better."

다양하게 표현할 수 있어요!

* 친구가 남자인 경우 He, Him, 여자인 경우 She, Her.

Then, he will feel better.
she
your friend

That will make him feel much better.
her
your friend

친구가 괜찮다고 손 잡아주네

시온맘's Pick

"She's holding your hand to tell you that it's okay."

다양하게 표현할 수 있어요!

* 친구가 남자인 경우 He, 여자인 경우 She.

He is holding your hand now, saying "It's okay" .
She
Your friend

He is holding your hand to tell you that it's okay.
She
Your friend

He is holding your hand to let you know that it's okay.
She
Your friend

나중에 친구가 미안하다고 사과하면, 너도 괜찮다고 해주렴

시온맘's Pick

"Next time when your friend says he is sorry to you, you could tell him it's okay, too."

다양하게 표현할 수 있어요!

* 친구가 남자인 경우 He, Him, 여자인 경우 She, Her.

Next time he says he is sorry, tell him "It's okay" too.
she / she / her
your friend

When he apologizes to you next time, you can also say "It's okay".
she / in the future,
your friend

Next time when he says he is sorry to you, you could tell him it's okay, too.
she / she / her
your friend

또 그러면 엄마 마음도 아플 거야

시온맘's Pick

"When it happens again, I'll be sad."

다양하게 표현할 수 있어요!

When you do that again, I'll be very sad.
really

I'll be (very / really) sad if it happens again.

I'll be (very / really) sad if you do that again.

When it happens again, I'll be (very / really) sad.

다시는 때리지 않겠다고 약속하자

시온맘's Pick

"I need you to promise me that you will keep your hands to yourself."

다양하게 표현할 수 있어요!

Promise (me) not to hit again.

Promise (me) to keep your hands to yourself.

Promise (me) that you will never hit your friends again.

Promise (me) that you will keep your hands to yourself.

I need you to promise me that you will keep your hands to yourself.

I need you to promise me that you will not hit your friends (ever) again.

다시는 그러면 안 된단다
다시는 그러지 않겠다고 약속하자

시온맘's Pick

"Promise me it will not happen ever again."

다양하게 표현할 수 있어요!

Promise me you'll never do this again.
Promise me that you won't do it again.
Promise me it will not happen (ever) again.

시온맘's Pick

"Can you promise me it will not happen ever again?"

다양하게 표현할 수 있어요!

(+ Can you - ?)
Promise me you'll never do this again.
Promise me that you won't do it again.
Promise me it will not happen (ever) again.

다시는 그러지 말자

시온맘's Pick

"Don't let this happen ever again."

다양하게 표현할 수 있어요!

Don't do (ever) it again.
this
that

Don't let it happen (ever) again.
this
that

I hope it does not happen (ever) again.
this
that

새끼손가락 걸고 약속!

시온맘's Pick

"Make a promise with your pinky."

다양하게 표현할 수 있어요!

Pinky swear.
promise.

It's a promise.

Make a pinky promise.

Promise (me) with your pinky.
little finger.

Make a promise with your pinky.
little finger.

친구도 장난감을 양보했었잖니

시온맘's Pick

"Remember that she shared her toy with you last time."

다양하게 표현할 수 있어요!

* 친구가 남자인 경우 He, His, 여자인 경우 She, Her.

He shared his toy with you before.
She her last time.
Your friend

He let you play with his toy before.
She her last time.
Your friend

Remember when he shared his toy with you?
she her
your friend

Remember that he shared his toy with you before?
she her last time?
your friend

뺏는 건 안 된단다

시온맘's Pick

"You shouldn't snatch things away from your friend."

다양하게 표현할 수 있어요!

* 친구가 남자인 경우 His, Him, 여자인 경우 Her.

Don't take it away.
snatch

It's not nice to take away his.
her.
toys.
belongings.
your friend's things.

It's not nice to take toys away from him.
things her.
your friend.

You shouldn't take toys away from him.
things her.
your friend.

You shouldn't snatch toys away from him.
things her.
your friend.

* 물건 Things * 장난감 Toys * 소유물 Belongings
* Take away : 빼앗다 * Snatch : 잡아채다, 잡아 뺏다

(너도) 규칙을 지켜야 한단다

시온맘's Pick

"You should stick to the rules."

다양하게 표현할 수 있어요!

You should (Also) mind the rules.
stick to
abide by

* Mind : ~을 지키다
* Stick to : (충실히) ~을 따르다
* Abide by : ~에 따라 행동하다

차례를 기다려야 하는 거야

시온맘's Pick

"You need to wait until you get your turn."

다양하게 표현할 수 있어요!

(+ Please)
Wait (for) your turn.

You should wait (for) your turn.
need to
have to

You should wait until it's your turn.
need to
have to

You should wait until you get your turn.
need to
have to

아직 네 차례가 아니란다

시온맘's Pick

"Your turn hasn't come yet."

다양하게 표현할 수 있어요!

It's not your turn yet.
Your turn hasn't come yet.

그 다음 네 차례란다

시온맘's Pick

"Your turn is coming up soon."

다양하게 표현할 수 있어요!

* 친구가 남자인 경우 Him, 여자인 경우 Her.

You're after him.
her.

You're (up) next.
Your turn is coming.
It's almost your turn.
It will be your turn soon.
Your turn is coming up soon.

기다려봐

시온맘's Pick

"Hold on a moment."

다양하게 표현할 수 있어요!

Wait.
Hold on.
Hang on.

Wait a minute.
a second.
a moment.
a little while.

Hold on a minute.
a second.
a moment.
a little while.

Hang on a minute.
a second.
a moment.
a little while.

조금만 기다리면 돼

시온맘's Pick

"You need to wait just a little longer."

다양하게 표현할 수 있어요!

You need to wait just a little longer.

You just need to wait a little bit.
a little while.

진정해, 기다려봐

시온맘's Pick

"Hold your horses."

다양하게 표현할 수 있어요!

Hold your water.
Hold your horses.

네 차례란다

시온맘's Pick

"Take your turn."

다양하게 표현할 수 있어요!

Take your turn.
It's your turn (now).

잘 기다렸네

시온맘's Pick

"You did a good job waiting."

다양하게 표현할 수 있어요!

You waited so well.
You did a good job waiting.

참을 줄도 알아야지, 잘했어

시온맘's Pick

"You need to learn to be patient. Great job."

다양하게 표현할 수 있어요!

You should learn to wait.
need to

You should learn to be patient.
need to

* 아래 정리된 표현들은 모두 "잘했다" 는 뜻을 가지고 있습니다.
위에 문장들 전이나 후에 아래 표현들 중 하나를 더하시면 됩니다.

* Nice
* Good
* Excellent.
* Great job.
* Well done.
* Two thumbs up.

* Good boy.
* Good girl.

* 자녀가 남자인 경우 Boy. 여자인 경우 Girl.

* You did a nice job.
good
great

* There's a good boy.
girl.

같이 놀아야지 나누면서 놀아야지

시온맘's Pick

"You need to play with those together."

다양하게 표현할 수 있어요!

You need to share.

You need to play with these together.
those

You need to share with others when you play together.

시온맘's Pick

"It's nice to play with those together."

이렇게도 표현할 수 있어요!

(You should -)
(You have to -)
(It's nice to -)
You need to share.

You need to play with these together.
those

You need to share with others when you play together.

가진 것을 나누는 것이 배려란다

시온맘's Pick

"Sharing is caring."

가진 것을 나눌수록 엄마는 네가 원하는 것을 더 사줄 거야

시온맘's Pick

"The more you share what you have, the more I'll buy you things you like."

다양하게 표현할 수 있어요!

The more you share with others, the more I'll buy you things you like.

The more you share what you have, the more I'll buy you things you like.

착하네, 나눌 줄도 알고

시온맘's Pick

"It's nice of you to know how to share."

다양하게 표현할 수 있어요!

It's (really / very) nice of you to know how to share.

잘했어. 기특해

시온맘's Pick

"Two thumbs up. I'm so proud of you."

다양하게 표현할 수 있어요!

* 자녀가 남자인 경우 Boy, 여자인 경우 Girl.

Nice. + *
Good. + *
Excellent. + *
Great job. + *
Well done. + *

Good boy. + *
girl. + *

Two thumbs up. + *

There's a good boy. + *
girl. + *

You did a nice job. + *
You did a good job. + *
You did a great job. + *

* I'm so proud of you.

사이좋게 지내보자

시온맘's Pick

"Be good friends with one another."

다양하게 표현할 수 있어요!

Be nice to each other.
Try to get along with your friend.
Be good friends with one another.

둘이 잘 지내니까 엄마가 기분이 좋네

시온맘's Pick

"I'm happy you're being nice to each other."

다양하게 표현할 수 있어요!

I'm glad you get along very well.
I'm happy you get along very well.

I'm glad you two are getting along.
I'm happy you two are getting along.

I'm glad you two are good friends.
I'm happy you two are good friends.

I'm glad you're being nice to each other.
I'm happy you're being nice to each other.

시온맘's Pick

"It's great to see that you're being nice to each other."

이렇게도 표현할 수 있어요!

(It's great to see that -)

I'm glad you get along very well.
I'm happy you get along very well.

I'm glad you two are getting along.
I'm happy you two are getting along.

I'm glad you two are good friends.
I'm happy you two are good friends.

I'm glad you're being nice to each other.
I'm happy you're being nice to each other.

티비 볼 때

When Watching TV

오늘 몇 개 보려고?

시온맘's Pick

"How many episodes will you watch?"

다양하게 표현할 수 있어요!

How many episodes will you watch?
How many episodes are you going to watch?

엄마 생각에 4개는 너무 많은 것 같구나 오늘은 2개만 보는 건 어때?

시온맘's Pick

"Four episodes seem too much. I think you should watch two for today."

다양하게 표현할 수 있어요!

I think four is too many. How about two?

Four episodes seem too much. I think you should watch two for today.

* 문장 속 숫자는 자유롭게 변경하여 사용하세요.

(약속한 시간) 시간 다 됐단다

시온맘's Pick

"It's time."

다양하게 표현할 수 있어요!

It's time.

Time's up.

It's time to stop watching the TV.

이제 끄자
그만 껐으면 좋겠네

시온맘's Pick

"Let's turn it off now."

다양하게 표현할 수 있어요!

Turn off the TV (now).

Let's turn it off (now).
the TV

It's time to turn it off.
the TV.

시온맘's Pick

"Why don't you turn it off now?"

다양하게 표현할 수 있어요!

(+ Why don't you - ?)
Turn off the TV (now).

(Why don't you - ?)
Let's turn it off (now).
the TV

It's time to turn it off.
the TV.

티비 그만 보렴
티비 이제 그만 봤으면 좋겠네

시온맘's Pick

"I think you should stop watching TV."

다양하게 표현할 수 있어요!

Stop watching TV.
I want you to stop watching TV.
I think you should stop watching TV.

시온맘's Pick

"You'd better stop watching TV."

이렇게도 표현할 수 있어요!

(You should -)
(You'd better -)
I want you to stop watching TV.
I think you should stop watching TV.

오늘 너무 많이 봤어

시온맘's Pick

"That's enough for today."

다양하게 표현할 수 있어요!

That's enough for today.

You've watched enough.
too much.

You've watched for a long time.

You've watched too many episodes today.

내일 마저 보자

시온맘's Pick

"You can watch the rest tomorrow."

다양하게 표현할 수 있어요!

You can finish it tomorrow.

You can continue (watching) tomorrow.

You can finish the rest (of the episode) tomorrow.
watch

벌써 한 시간이나 지났구나

시온맘's Pick

"It's already been an hour."

다양하게 표현할 수 있어요!

It's already been an hour.
one hour.

It already passed an hour.
one hour.

An hour has (already) passed.
One hour

* 문장 속 시간은 자유롭게 변경하여 사용하세요.

10분만 보렴

시온맘's Pick

"Only for ten minutes."

다양하게 표현할 수 있어요!

Just ten minutes.
Only for ten minutes.
I will give you ten minutes.
You can watch it for ten minutes.

* 문장 속 시간은 자유롭게 변경하여 사용하세요.

아직 안 끝났니?

시온맘's Pick

"Has this episode not ended?"

다양하게 표현할 수 있어요!

Isn't it over yet?
done

Has the show not ended?
this episode

그것까지만 보렴

시온맘's Pick

"That should be your last episode."

다양하게 표현할 수 있어요!

That's the last one.
episode.

That should be your last episode.

소리 좀 줄이자

시온맘's Pick

"Lower the volume."

다양하게 표현할 수 있어요!

(Let's) Turn it down.
(Let's) Lower the volume.
(Let's) Turn the volume down.

TV 앞에 누우면 안 된단다

시온맘's Pick

"You had better not lie down in front of the TV."

다양하게 표현할 수 있어요!

* 조언의 강도 조절

Should not < had better not < must not

Don't lie down in front of TV.

It's not good to lie down in front of the TV.

You shouldn't lie down in front of the TV.
had better not
mustn't

너무 가까이 앉았네

시온맘's Pick

"You're sitting too close to the TV."

다양하게 표현할 수 있어요!

You're sitting too close (to the TV).

좀 더 떨어져 앉으렴

시온맘's Pick

"Sit away from the TV."

다양하게 표현할 수 있어요!

Sit a little further.
Sit away from the TV.

뒤로 오렴

시온맘's Pick

"Please move further."

다양하게 표현할 수 있어요!

(+ Please)

Sit back.

Move back.
further.

Scoot back a little.

* Scoot : 서둘러 가다, 서둘러 떠나다
* Scoot back : '빨리 뒤로 가'라는 뜻을 가진 슬랭

너무 가까이 있구나

시온맘's Pick

"You are way too close to the TV."

다양하게 표현할 수 있어요!

You are (way) too close to the TV.

뒤로 좀 물러나렴, 너무 가까이 있구나

시온맘's Pick

"Why don't you scoot back a little, you're too close?"

다양하게 표현할 수 있어요!

Why don't you move further, you're too close?
scoot back a little,

시온맘's Pick

"You should scoot back a little, you're too close."

이렇게도 표현할 수 있어요!

(You should -)
Why don't you move further, you're too close?
scoot back a little,

TV 너무 가까이서 보면 눈 버린단다

시온맘's Pick

"Sitting too close to the TV is going to ruin your eyes."

다양하게 표현할 수 있어요!

Sitting too close to the TV is not good for your eyes.
eyesight.

Sitting too close to the TV will ruin your eyes.
is going to

Sitting too close to the TV will damage your eyesight.
is going to

If you sit too close to the TV, you will ruin your eyes.
are going to

If you sit too close to the TV, you will damage your eyesight.
are going to

많이 보는 것은 눈에 좋지 않단다

시온맘's Pick

"Watching too much TV is going to damage your eyesight."

다양하게 표현할 수 있어요!

Watching too much TV will ruin your eyes.
is going to

Watching too much TV is not good for eyesight.
your eyes.

Watching too much TV will damage your eyesight.
is going to

If you watch TV for too long, you will ruin your eyes.
are going to

If you watch TV for too long, you will damage your eyesight.
are going to

시력이 나빠질 수 있어

시온맘's Pick

"Your eyesight will be damaged."

다양하게 표현할 수 있어요!

You can worsen your eyesight.

Your eyesight will be ruined.
damaged.

Your eyesight will become worse.

시력이 나빠지면, 사물이 흐릿하게 보인단다

시온맘's Pick

"If your eyesight gets worse, things at a distance become blurry."

다양하게 표현할 수 있어요!

If your eyesight gets worse, your vision gets blurry.

If your eyesight gets worse, things at a distance become blurry.

You will start to see things with a blurred vision when your eyesight gets worse.

* Blurry : 흐릿한
* Blurred : 흐릿한, 희미한

시력이 나빠지면, 멀리 있는 사물이 잘 안 보인단다

시온맘's Pick

"If your eyesight gets worse, you can't see things at a distance very well."

다양하게 표현할 수 있어요!

If your eyesight gets worse, you can't see things at a distance that / very well.

If your eyesight gets worse, it's hard to see things (that are) far away.

시력을 보호하려면, 적절한 거리를 유지해야 한단다

시온맘's Pick

"To protect your eyesight, you should keep your distance from TV."

다양하게 표현할 수 있어요!

To protect your vision, you should keep your distance from TV.
eyesight, maintain a distance

To maintain good eyesight, you should keep a distance from TV.

네가 좋아하는 프로그램이니?

시온맘's Pick

“Is that a show you like to watch?”

다양하게 표현할 수 있어요!

Is this your favorite show?
that

Is this a show you like to watch?
that

Is this one of your favorite shows?
that

Is this one of the favorite shows you like to watch?
that

재밌어?

시온맘's Pick

"Is the show fun?"

다양하게 표현할 수 있어요!

Is the show fun?
How's the show?
Are you enjoying the show?

재밌게 잘 보네

시온맘's Pick

"You seem to be enjoying the show."

다양하게 표현할 수 있어요!

You seem to be enjoying the show.

You seem like you're enjoying the show.

(아이가 TV를 보고 있는 상황)

엄마도 같이 봐야겠다

시온맘's Pick

"I should watch it with you."

손가락 빨 때

When Sucking on Fingers

손가락 빨면 안 돼
손가락 빨지 마렴

시온맘's Pick

"No finger sucking."

다양하게 표현할 수 있어요!

(+ Please 안 됨)
No fingers.
No finger sucking.

(+ Please)
Don't suck (on) your finger.
Stop sucking (on) your fingers.

입에 넣은 손가락 빼렴
입에 넣은 손가락 빼보자

시온맘's Pick

"Let's keep your fingers away from your mouth."

다양하게 표현할 수 있어요!

(+ Please)

Take your fingers out of your mouth.

(+ Please 안 됨)

Let's keep your fingers out of your mouth.
away from

손가락 빠는 거 안 좋아

시온맘's Pick

"Sucking on your fingers is not a good thing to do."

다양하게 표현할 수 있어요!

Finger sucking is bad for you.
Sucking (on) your fingers

It's not good to suck (on) your finger.

Finger sucking is not a good thing to do.
Sucking (on) your fingers

손가락 빠는 거 안 좋은 습관이란다

시온맘's Pick

"It's a bad habit."

다양하게 표현할 수 있어요!

It's not a good habit.
It's a (very) bad habit.

나쁜 습관은 버리자

시온맘's Pick

"Drop your bad habits."

다양하게 표현할 수 있어요!

Fix the bad habits.
your

Drop the bad habits.
your

Give up the bad habits.
your

Get rid of the bad habits.
your

시온맘's Pick

"Let's drop your bad habits."

이렇게도 표현할 수 있어요!

(+ Let's -)
(+ Please)

Fix the bad habits.
your

Drop the bad habits.
your

Give up the bad habits.
your

Get rid of the bad habits.
your

나쁜 습관은 버려야 해

시온맘's Pick

"You must drop your bad habits."

다양하게 표현할 수 있어요!

You must drop the bad habits.
your

You must give up the bad habits.
your

You must try to fix the bad habits.
your

You must get rid of the bad habits.
your

시온맘's Pick

"You had better drop your bad habits."

이렇게도 표현할 수 있어요!

(- should -)
(- need to -)
(- have to -)
(- had better -)
You must drop the bad habits.
your

You must give up the bad habits.
your

You must try to fix the bad habits.
your

You must get rid of the bad habits.
your

나쁜 습관을 고치는 건 참 어렵지만, 계속 노력해야 한단다

시온맘's Pick

"Breaking a bad habit isn't easy, but you should keep trying."

다양하게 표현할 수 있어요!

Fixing a bad habit isn't easy, but you should keep trying.
Breaking

It may not be easy to fix a bad habit, but you should keep trying.
break

Of course, it's not easy to fix a bad habit, you should keep trying.
break

* should 자리에 대체 가능한 조동사들입니다.
* must
* have to
* need to

손가락 자꾸 빨면 녹는다잉

시온맘's Pick

"If you keep sucking your fingers, they will melt like ice cream."

다양하게 표현할 수 있어요!

If you keep sucking (on) your fingers, they will melt like candy.
ice cream.

아빠한테 이른다잉

시온맘's Pick

"I will call daddy and tell on you."

다양하게 표현할 수 있어요!

I will tell daddy.

I will call daddy and tell on you.

* 문장 속 목적어는 자유롭게 변경하여 사용하세요.

주사 맞아야겠네

시온맘's Pick

"Maybe you need to take a shot."

다양하게 표현할 수 있어요!

You may have to get a shot.
take

Maybe you need to get a shot.
take

I think you may have to get a shot.
take

경찰 아저씨 불러야겠네

시온맘's Pick

"I should tell the policeman."

다양하게 표현할 수 있어요!

I should call the police.
tell policeman.
police officer.

시온맘's Pick

"I think I should tell the policeman."

이렇게도 표현할 수 있어요!

(+ I think -)
I should call the police.
tell policeman.
police officer.

배 아파서 병원 갔던 거 기억나?

시온맘's Pick

"Remember going to see a doctor because of a tummy ache?"

다양하게 표현할 수 있어요!

Remember going to a doctor because of a tummy ache?
to see a doctor / stomach ache?

Remember (when) you had to go to a doctor because of your tummy ache?
see a doctor / stomach ache?

Remember (when) you had a tummy ache and had to go to a doctor?
stomach ache / see a doctor?

시온맘's Pick

"Do you remember going to see a doctor because of a tummy ache?"

이렇게도 표현할 수 있어요!

(Do you remember - ?)
Remember going to a doctor because of a tummy ache?
to see a doctor / stomach ache?

Remember (when) you had to go to a doctor because of your tummy ache?
see a doctor / stomach ache?

Remember (when) you had a tummy ache and had to go to a doctor?
stomach ache / see a doctor?

* 미국에서는 '병원을 간다'고 할 때, 큰 질병이 아닌 경우, 'go to the hospital'보다 'see a doctor' 또는 'go to a doctor'을 더 많이 사용합니다.

손가락 빨면 또 배 아프단다

시온맘's Pick

"Sucking on your finger can cause a stomach ache."

다양하게 표현할 수 있어요!

You can hurt your tummy.
stomach.

Sucking (on) your fingers will get you sick.

Sucking (on) your finger can cause a tummy ache.
stomach ache.

If you suck (on) your fingers, you'll get a tummy ache.
stomach ache.

You can get a tummy ache from sucking (on) your fingers.
stomach ache

나쁜 벌레들이 몸으로 들어가면 배가 아프기 시작해

시온맘's Pick

"When bad bugs go inside your body, you could get sick."

다양하게 표현할 수 있어요!

You could get sick when germs go inside your body.
bad bugs

When germs go inside your body, you could get sick.
bad bugs

손에 항상 균들이 살고 있단다
손에 항상 나쁜 벌레가 살고 있단다

시온맘's Pick

"There are bad bugs called germs on your hands."

다양하게 표현할 수 있어요!

There're always germs (living) on your hands.
bad bugs

There are bad bugs called germs (living) on your hands.

손은 항상 더럽단다

시온맘's Pick

"Your hands are always dirty."

엄마는 우리 아들 / 딸이 아프지 않았으면 좋겠어

시온맘's Pick

"I hope you are not coming down with something."

다양하게 표현할 수 있어요!

I (always) hope you are not sick.

I (always) hope you won't get sick.

I (always) hope everything is fine with you.
okay
all right

I (always) hope you are not coming down with something.

주사 또 맞고 싶어? 아니지?

시온맘's Pick

"You don't want the needle right? No, right?"

다양하게 표현할 수 있어요!

You don't want the shot right? + *
needle

Do you want to get another shot? + *

* Do you?
* No, right?
* You don't, right?

그럼 우리 어떻게 해야 할까?

시온맘's Pick

"Then what should we do?"

다양하게 표현할 수 있어요!

Then what should we do?
What should we do, then?

손 빨면 안 되겠지?
손가락 빨면 안 되겠지?

시온맘's Pick

"You shouldn't suck your fingers, right?"

다양하게 표현할 수 있어요!

You shouldn't suck (on) your hands, right?
fingers,

시온맘's Pick

"You had better not suck your fingers, right?"

* 조언의 강도 조절

Should not < had better not < must not

이렇게도 표현할 수 있어요!

(- mustn't -)
(- had better not -)
You shouldn't suck (on) your hands, right?
fingers,

손가락 안 빨겠다고 약속할 수 있지?

시온맘's Pick

"Promise me you won't suck on your finger, will you?"

다양하게 표현할 수 있어요!

Can you promise not to suck (on) your finger?

Promise me (that) you won't suck (on) your finger, will you?

못하겠다고 떼쓸 때

When Throwing a Tantrum

끝까지 마저 다 해볼까

시온맘's Pick

"Do this all the way."

다양하게 표현할 수 있어요!

Do it all the way.
this

Finish it (all the way).
this

Get it done (all the way)
this

Get it finished (all the way).
this

시온맘's Pick

"Why don't you **do this all the way?**"

이렇게도 표현할 수 있어요!

(+ Let's-)
(+ Please)
(+ You should -)
(+ You need to -)
(+ You have to -)
(+ Why don't you - ?)

Do it all the way.
this

Finish it (all the way).
this

Get it done (all the way)
this

Get it finished (all the way).
this

계속 해보는 게 어때

시온맘's Pick

"Let's carry on the good work."

다양하게 표현할 수 있어요!

Let's go on.
Let's keep trying.
Let's keep going.
Let's keep working on it.
Let's keep up the good work.
Let's carry on the good work.
Let's (continue to) work on it.

시온맘's Pick

"Why don't you carry on the good work?"

이렇게도 표현할 수 있어요!

(Why don't you - ?)
Let's go on.
Let's keep trying.
Let's keep going.
Let's keep working on it.
Let's keep up the good work.
Let's carry on the good work.
Let's (continue to) work on it.

그렇게 어렵지 않아

시온맘's Pick

"It's not that hard as you think."

다양하게 표현할 수 있어요!

(It's) Easy! Peasy!
(It's) Easy! Peasy! Lemon squeezy!

It's not too hard (as you think).
difficult

It's not that hard (as you think).
difficult

쉬워서 금방 할 수 있단다

시온맘's Pick

"It's not very hard. You can do it in a short time."

다양하게 표현할 수 있어요!

It's easy. You can do it quickly.

It's not very hard. You can do it in a short time.

I'm sure you can do it right away because it's easy.
not that hard.

이거 혼자 잘 했잖아

시온맘's Pick

"You got it all by yourself."

다양하게 표현할 수 있어요!

You did it alone.
on your own.

You did it without any help.

You got it (all) by yourself.

You did this (all) by yourself.

시온맘's Pick

"You got it all by yourself before."

이렇게도 표현할 수 있어요!

You did it alone (before / last time).
on your own.

You did it without any help (before / last time).

You got it (all) by yourself (before / last time).

You did this (all) by yourself (before / last time).

혼자 할 수 있는 거란다

시온맘's Pick

"You can manage it on your own."

다양하게 표현할 수 있어요!

You can do it yourself.
by yourself.
on your own.

You can manage it yourself.
by yourself.
on your own.

You can do it without (any) help.

할 수 있는 만큼만 해보렴

시온맘's Pick

"You can do as much as you are able to do."

다양하게 표현할 수 있어요!

You can do it as best as you can.
could.

You can do it as long as you can.
could.

You can do (it) as much as you can.
could.

You can do as much as you feel like doing.

You can do (it) as much as you'd like to (do).

You can do (it) as much as you are able to (do).

시온맘's Pick

"Do it as much as you are able to do."

이렇게도 표현할 수 있어요!

(Do it -)

You can do it as best as you can.
could.

You can do it as long as you can.
could.

You can do (it) as much as you can.
could.

You can do (it) as much as you'd like to (do).

You can do (it) as much as you are able to (do).

(Do -)

You can do as much as you feel like doing.

도움이 필요하면 말해

시온맘's Pick

"Let me know if you are in need of help."

다양하게 표현할 수 있어요!

Tell me if you need (my) help.
Let me know

Tell me if you are in need of help.
Let me know

시온맘's Pick

"You can tell me if you are in need of help."

이렇게도 표현할 수 있어요!

You can tell me if you need (my) help.
You can tell me if you are in need of help.

엄마가 도와줄게

시온맘's Pick

"Let me give you a hand."

다양하게 표현할 수 있어요!

I'll help you (out).
I can
Let me

I'll give you a hand.
I can
Let me

I'll (help you) take care of it.
I can
Let me

(지금은 엄마가 도와줄게)

그 다음부턴 혼자 잘할 수 있을 거야

시온맘's Pick

"Mommy will help you this time. Next time, you can do a lot better."

다양하게 표현할 수 있어요!

* 엄마가 아이에게 자신을 표현하는 경우, 문장의 주어로 I, Mom보다는 Mommy를 더 많이 사용합니다. 더 친근한 느낌을 담고 있기 때문입니다.

* (I will help you this time.)
  Mommy

* (This time, I will help you.)
  Mommy

* + Then, you can do it better (than before / now).
  Next time, will

* + Then, you can do a lot better (than before / now).
  Next time, will much

* + Then, you can be great (when you are) on your own.
  Next time, will
  will be able to

* + Then, you can be better (when you are) on your own.
  Next time will
  will be able to

* + Then, you can do great (when you are) on your own.
  Next time will
  will be able to

* + Then, you can do (it) better (when you are) on your own.
  Next time will
  will be able to

* + Then, you can do a good job (when you are) on your own.
  Next time, will
  will be able to

* + Then, you can do a great job (when you are) on your own.
  Next time, will
  will be able to

한 번 해보자

시온맘's Pick

"Let's have a try at it."

다양하게 표현할 수 있어요!

Let's try (it).
Let's go for it.
Let's have a try.
Let's give it a go.
Let's give it a try.
Let's give it a whirl.
Let's have a try at it.
Let's make it happen.

해볼 만해

시온맘's Pick

"It's worth trying."

다양하게 표현할 수 있어요!

It's a challenge.
It's worth a try.
It's worth trying.
It's not that bad.

다시 해보자

시온맘's Pick

"Let's just do that one more time."

다양하게 표현할 수 있어요!

Let's start over.

Let's give it another try.

Let's try (once) again.
one more time.

Let's try it (once) again.
one more time.

Let's do it (once) again.
one more time.

Let's just do that (once) again.
one more time.

시온맘's Pick

"You can just do that one more time."

이렇게도 표현할 수 있어요!

You can start over.

You can give it another try.

You can try (once) again.
one more time.

You can try it (once) again.
one more time.

You can do it (once) again.
one more time.

You can just do that (once) again.
one more time.

어려운 것도 할 수 있어

시온맘's Pick

"You are ready for something more."

다양하게 표현할 수 있어요!

You can do hard things.
You can do more than that.
You are ready for something more.

시온맘's Pick

"I believe that you are ready for something more."

이렇게도 표현할 수 있어요!

(+ I believe that -)
You can do hard things.
You can do more than that.
You are ready for something more.

집에 안 들어가려 할 때

When Refusing to Go Back Home

더 놀고 싶구나?

시온맘's Pick

"Do you want to play more?"

날이 점점 어두워지네

시온맘's Pick

"The sun is going down."

다양하게 표현할 수 있어요!

It's getting dark.

It's starting to get darker.

The sun is setting.
going down.

밖이 완전 깜깜하네

시온맘's Pick

"It's dark out."

다양하게 표현할 수 있어요!

It's dark out.
It's very dark outside.

집에 갈 시간이구나

시온맘's Pick

"Time to head back home now."

다양하게 표현할 수 있어요!

(It's) Time to go home (now).
head

We should go back home (now).
head

(It's) Time to go back home (now).
head

이제 들어가자구나

시온맘's Pick

"Let's head inside."

다양하게 표현할 수 있어요!

Let's go back.
head

Let's go inside.
head

Let's go back home.
head

들어가서 밥 먹자

시온맘's Pick

"Let's head inside and eat."

다양하게 표현할 수 있어요!

Let's go back and eat.
head

Let's go inside and eat.
head

Let's go back home and eat.
head

이제 들어가서 씻고 자야지

시온맘's Pick

"Now you need to get cleaned and get ready for bed."

다양하게 표현할 수 있어요!

Now you should (go) get cleaned and get ready for bed.
need to

It's time for you to go back, get cleaned, and get ready for bed.

친구들도 다 집에 가네

시온맘's Pick

"Your friends are leaving."

다양하게 표현할 수 있어요!

Everyone is leaving.

(All of) Your friends are leaving.

시온맘's Pick

"Your friends are heading back home."

이렇게도 표현할 수 있어요!

* leaving 자리에 대신 사용할 수 있는 표현들입니다.

* going back
* going home
* heading home
* heading back home

Everyone is leaving.

(All of) Your friends are leaving.

우리 내일 와서 또 놀자구나

시온맘's Pick

"Let's come back and play again tomorrow."

다양하게 표현할 수 있어요!

Let's come again tomorrow and play here.
Let's come back and play again tomorrow.

시온맘's Pick

"You can come back and play again tomorrow."

이렇게도 표현할 수 있어요!

(You can -?)
(Why don't we -?)
Let's come again tomorrow and play here.
Let's come back and play again tomorrow.

밖에 오래 있으면 안 돼

시온맘's Pick

"Let's not stay out long."

다양하게 표현할 수 있어요!

Let's not stay out (for) long.
outside

You can't stay out (for) long.
outside

You shouldn't stay out (for) long.
outside

* for long을 대신할 수 있는 표현들입니다.

* too long
* for a long time

날이 너무 춥단다

시온맘's Pick

"It's icy cold outside."

다양하게 표현할 수 있어요!

It's chilly out.
today.
outside.

It's freezing out.
today.
outside.

It's icy cold out.
too today.
outside.

날이 추워지는 것 같네

시온맘's Pick

"It's getting cold."

다양하게 표현할 수 있어요!

It's getting chilly.
It's getting cold (now).
The weather's getting cold.

날이 너무 덥구나

시온맘's Pick

"It's burning hot today."

다양하게 표현할 수 있어요!

It's muggy out.
today.
outside.

It's (too) hot out.
today.
outside.

It's burning (hot) out.
today.
outside.

It's steaming (hot) out.
today.
outside.

감기에 걸릴 수 있단다

시온맘's Pick

"You can catch a cold easily."

다양하게 표현할 수 있어요!

You can get a cold.
catch

You can get a cold easily.
catch

시온맘's Pick

"You could catch a cold easily."

이렇게도 표현할 수 있어요!

(You may -)
(You could -)
You can get a cold.
catch

You can get a cold easily.
catch

감기 걸리면 어떻게 되지? 병원 가서 주사 맞아야 해

시온맘's Pick

"What happens when you catch a cold? You need to go to the doctor to get a shot."

다양하게 표현할 수 있어요!

What happens when you get a cold? You have to go to the doctor to get a shot.
have / catch (for "get") · need (for "have")

What do you have to do if you get a cold? You have to go and see a doctor to get a shot.
have / catch (for "get") · need (for "have")

오늘 많이 놀았어
오늘 놀만큼 놀았잖니

시온맘's Pick

"You've hung out for as long as you wanted today."

다양하게 표현할 수 있어요!

You played enough today.

You had enough play time today.

You've played as much as you could.

You had enough time to have fun today.

Haven't you had enough play time today?

You've hung out for as long as you wanted today.

말 잘 들어서 예쁘다

시온맘's Pick

"You are showing good behavior."

다양하게 표현할 수 있어요!

You are so well-behaved.
You are behaving so well.
You are showing good behavior.
You are doing a good job listening to me.
great / mommy.

엄마가 맛있는 거 해줄게

시온맘's Pick

"I will make something yummy for you."

다양하게 표현할 수 있어요!

I will fix something yummy for you.
make delicious
cook

시온맘's Pick

"Let me make something yummy for you."

이렇게도 표현할 수 있어요!

(Let me -)
I will fix something yummy for you.
make delicious
cook

엄마가 맛있는 거 사줄게

시온맘's Pick

"I will take you out to go get something delicious."

다양하게 표현할 수 있어요!

I will get you something yummy.
buy delicious.

I will get something yummy for you.
buy delicious.

I will take you out to go get something yummy.
delicious.

시온맘's Pick

"Let me take you out to go get something delicious."

이렇게도 표현할 수 있어요!

Let me get you something yummy.
buy delicious.

Let me get something yummy for you.
buy delicious.

Let me take you out to go get something yummy.
delicious.

엄마랑 같이 맛있는 거 먹으러 가자구나

시온맘's Pick

"Let's go eat something delicious."

다양하게 표현할 수 있어요!

Let's eat out.

Let's go eat something yummy.
delicious.

시온맘's Pick

"Why don't we go eat something delicious?"

이렇게도 표현할 수 있어요!

Why don't we eat out?

Why don't we go eat something yummy?
delicious?

계속 놀고 싶어 할 때

When a Child Wants to Continue to Play

그럼 엄마가 10분만 기다릴게

시온맘's Pick

"Then I will give you 10 minutes."

다양하게 표현할 수 있어요!

Then I will wait for 10 minutes.
Then I will give you 10 minutes more.

* 문장 속 시간은 자유롭게 변경하여 사용하세요.

이제 네 할 일 하렴

시온맘's Pick

"Go and do what you need to do."

다양하게 표현할 수 있어요!

Now do what you should do.
need to
have to

Go and do what you should do.
need to
have to

잠깐만 한다고 했잖니

시온맘's Pick

"You told me you would do it only for a minute."

다양하게 표현할 수 있어요!

You promised only to do it for a bit.
a little bit.
a short time.
a little while.

You said you would do it (only) for a bit.
a little bit.
a short time.
a little while.

You told me (that) you would do it (only) for a bit.
a minute
a little bit.
a short time.
a little while.

약속했잖니

시온맘's Pick

"You promised."

이거 하겠다고 약속하지 않았니?

시온맘's Pick

"Didn't you tell me you were going to do this?"

다양하게 표현할 수 있어요!

Didn't you promise me to do this?

You promised to do this. Didn't you?

Didn't you say you were going to do this?
tell me

약속은 지켜야 한단다

시온맘's Pick

"Remember, a promise is meant to be kept."

다양하게 표현할 수 있어요!

Remember, a promise is meant to be kept.
You should keep the promise (you made).

엄마가 네 이야기를 듣지 않으면 네 기분이 어떻겠니?

시온맘's Pick

"How would you like it if mommy wasn't listening to you?"

다양하게 표현할 수 있어요!

How would you feel if I didn't listen to you?
like it mommy

How would you feel if I wasn't listening to you?
like it mommy

* 엄마가 아이에게 자신을 표현하는 경우, 문장의 주어로 I, Mom보다는 Mommy를 더 많이 사용합니다. 더 친근한 느낌을 담고 있기 때문입니다.

엄마가 너와의 약속을 지키지 않으면 네 기분이 어떻겠니?

시온맘's Pick

"How would you like it if mommy didn't keep her promise with you?"

다양하게 표현할 수 있어요!

How would you feel if I didn't keep my promise with you?
like it mommy her promise

How would you feel if I didn't keep the promise I made to you?
like it mommy she

* 엄마가 아이에게 자신을 표현하는 경우, 문장의 주어로 I, Mom보다는 Mommy를 더 많이 사용합니다. 더 친근한 느낌을 담고 있기 때문입니다.
* Mommy를 사용할 경우, 문장 안에서 my promise는 her promise로 바꾸어주세요.
* Mommy를 사용할 경우, 문장 안에서 I는 she로 바꾸어주세요.

약속 잘 지켜서 예쁘다

시온맘's Pick

"I'm proud of you for keeping your promise."

다양하게 표현할 수 있어요!

I'm glad you kept your promise.
happy

I'm proud of you for keeping your promise.

It makes me very happy to see you keep your promise.

말 잘 들어서 예쁘다

시온맘's Pick

"You are doing a great job listening to mommy."

다양하게 표현할 수 있어요!

You are so well-behaved.
You are behaving so well.
You are showing good behavior.
You are doing a good job listening to me.
great mommy.

* 엄마가 아이에게 자신을 표현하는 경우, 문장의 목적어로 Me, Mom보다는 Mommy를 더 많이 사용합니다. 더 친근한 느낌을 담고 있기 때문입니다.

무례하게 행동할 때

When a Child is Being Disrespectful

왜 이렇게 버릇없이 행동하는 거니?

시온맘's Pick

"Why are you being so disrespectful to mommy?"

다양하게 표현할 수 있어요!

Why are you being so rude to me?
disrespectful mommy?

* 엄마가 아이에게 자신을 표현하는 경우, 문장의 목적어로 Me, Mom보다는 Mommy를 더 많이 사용합니다. 더 친근한 느낌을 담고 있기 때문입니다.

예의 바르게 행동하자

시온맘's Pick

"Behave yourself."

다양하게 표현할 수 있어요!

(+ Please)
Be polite.
Behave yourself.
Use your manners.
Have some manners.
Be at your best behavior.

시온맘's Pick

"You should behave yourself."

이렇게도 표현할 수 있어요!

(+ Try to -)
(+ You should -)
(+ Please try to -)
Be polite.
Behave yourself.
Use your manners.
Have some manners.
Be at your best behavior.

이건 아주 무례한 행동이란다

시온맘's Pick

"Such behavior is impolite."

다양하게 표현할 수 있어요!

It's not polite.
It's (very) rude.
It's (very) impolite.
Such behavior is not polite.
(very) rude.
(very) impolite.

예의를 지키는 건 중요해

시온맘's Pick

"It's important to be at your best behavior."

다양하게 표현할 수 있어요!

Being polite is important.
It's important to be polite.

Behaving yourself is important.
It's important to behave yourself.

Keeping your manners is important.
It's important to keep your manners.

It's important to have some manners.
Having good manners is important.

It's important to be at your best behavior.
Being at your best behavior is important.

예의를 갖추는 것은 바른 자세이기도 하지만, 우리가 꼭 지켜야하는 것이기도 하단다.

시온맘's Pick

"Being respectful is more than simply behaving yourself, but it is the right thing to do."

다양하게 표현할 수 있어요!

It's not only good manners, but the right thing to do.

Being polite / Being respectful / Having good manners is more than simply behaving yourself, but it is the right thing to do.

인사 드리렴

시온맘's Pick

"Tell her 안녕하세요!"

다양하게 표현할 수 있어요!

* 아이가 인사를 드리는 대상에 따라 목적어를 바꾸어주시면 됩니다.
* 상대가 여자인 경우 Her, 남자인 경우 Him.

Tell him 안녕하세요!
her
them

Say 안녕하세요 to him.
her
them

인사 드렸니?

시온맘's Pick

"Did you tell her '안녕하세요'?"

다양하게 표현할 수 있어요!

* 아이가 인사를 드리는 대상에 따라 목적어를 바꾸어주시면 됩니다.
* 상대가 여자인 경우 Her, 남자인 경우 Him.

Did you say "**안녕하세요**" to him?
her?
them?

Did you tell him "**안녕하세요**"?
her
them

항상 먼저 인사하렴

시온맘's Pick

"You should always greet others when you first see them."

다양하게 표현할 수 있어요!

* 아이가 인사를 드리는 대상에 따라 목적어를 바꾸어주시면 됩니다.
* 상대가 여자인 경우 Her, 남자인 경우 Him.

Always greet (others) first when you see him.
her.
them.

You should always greet others when you first see him.
her.
them.

공손하게 인사해보자

시온맘's Pick

"Let's greet them politely."

다양하게 표현할 수 있어요!

* 아이가 인사를 드리는 대상에 따라 목적어를 바꾸어주시면 됩니다.
* 상대가 여자인 경우 Her, 남자인 경우 Him.

Let's greet him politely.
her
them

시온맘's Pick

"You should greet them politely."

이렇게도 표현할 수 있어요!

You should greet him politely.
her
them

두 손을 배꼽에

시온맘's Pick

"Put your hands on your belly button. Do it properly."

다양하게 표현할 수 있어요!

Hands on your belly. + *

Put both hands on your belly button. + *
your hands

* Do it politely.
properly.

배꼽인사 해야지

시온맘's Pick

"You should bow down."

다양하게 표현할 수 있어요!

You should bow (down).

Put both hands on your belly and bow (down).
your hands

장난치지 말고

시온맘's Pick

"Please quit goofing off."

다양하게 표현할 수 있어요!

(+ Please)

Don't goof off.
Don't joke around.
Don't play around.
Don't goof around.
Don't horse around.

(+ Please)

Stop goofing off.
Quit goofing off.

Stop joking around.
Quit joking around.

Stop horsing around.
Quit horsing around.

Stop playing around.
Quit playing around.

Stop goofing around.
Quit goofing around.

* 위 문장들 전이나 후에 "Mommy said" 또는 "I said"를 붙이면 조금 더 단호한 느낌이 날 수 있습니다.
* Goof off : 빈둥거리다(할 일을 안 하고 시간을 낭비하는 뉘앙스)
* Horse around : 법석을 떨다(말의 행동과 같이 법석을 떨면서 장난치는 뉘앙스)

큰 소리로 인사하렴

시온맘's Pick

"Greet them with a louder voice."

다양하게 표현할 수 있어요!

* 아이가 인사를 드리는 대상에 따라 목적어를 바꾸어주시면 됩니다.
* 상대가 여자인 경우 Her, 남자인 경우 Him.

Come on. Louder.
Can you say it louder?
Why don't you say it louder?
Greet him with a louder voice.
her
them

인사 잘하네

시온맘's Pick

"You're doing a good job greeting people."

다양하게 표현할 수 있어요!

You know how to greet others well.
You're doing a good job (with) greeting people.

착하구나

시온맘's Pick

"What a good girl!"

다양하게 표현할 수 있어요!

* 자녀가 아들인 경우 Boy, 딸인 경우 girl.

What a good boy!
girl!

공손하게 말하는 거 잊지 말자

시온맘's Pick

"Speak nicely."

다양하게 표현할 수 있어요!

Speak nicely.
politely.

Don't forget to say, "Please".
Don't forget to use the magic words.

* 아래 표현들을 the magic words라고 합니다.

* 'Please'
* 'I'm sorry'
* 'Thank you'
* 'Excuse me'
* 'You're welcome'

엄마 옆에 있자

시온맘's Pick

"Stay right here by mommy."

다양하게 표현할 수 있어요!

* 엄마가 아이에게 자신을 표현하는 경우, 문장의 목적어로 Me, Mom보다는 Mommy를 더 많이 사용합니다. 더 친근한 느낌을 담고 있기 때문입니다.

Stay by my side.

Stay near me.
Stay next to mommy.

Stay up here by me.
right mommy.

조용히 놀고 있자

시온맘's Pick

"Lower down while you play."

다양하게 표현할 수 있어요!

(+ Try to -)
Play quietly.

Stay quiet as you play.
while

Lower down as you play.
while

어른들 이야기하고 있으니, 조금만 기다리렴

시온맘's Pick

"Hang on a little while. I will be with you shortly."

다양하게 표현할 수 있어요!

Be patient. We are talking (right now).
Be patient. I will be with you (shortly).

* Be patient. 자리에 다음 아래 표현들을 대신 사용할 수 있습니다.
Wait. Hold on. Hang on.

Wait a minute.
a second.
a moment.
a little while.

Hold on a minute.
a second.
a moment.
a little while.

Hang on a minute.
a second.
a moment.
a little while.

오늘 정말 잘했어

시온맘's Pick

"You behaved very well today."

다양하게 표현할 수 있어요!

Well done today.
Excellent job today.
You behaved very well today.

(You did a) Nice job today.
Good
Great

Two thumbs up, you did good today.
great

어른들 이야기 끝날 때까지 기다리느라 힘들었지. 기특해

시온맘's Pick

"Thank you for your patience while the adults finished their conversation."

다양하게 표현할 수 있어요!

Thanks for waiting for us to be done talking.
Thank you

Thanks for waiting for us to finish our conversation.
Thank you

Thanks for your patience while the adults finished their conversation.
Thank you

아이의 생각 묻기
Asking for Their Thoughts/Opinions

마음 좀 풀렸니?
지금은 좀 어때?
기분 좀 좋아졌니?

시온맘's Pick

"Are you in a better mood?"

다양하게 표현할 수 있어요!

How about now?

Do you feel fine (now)?
okay

How do you feel (now)?
How are you feeling (now)?

Are you feeling better (now)?
Do you feel (any) better (now)?

Are you in a better mood (now)?

엄마와 대화하면서 속상한 마음 좀 풀렸니?

시온맘's Pick

"Now that we talked, are you in a better mood?"

다양하게 표현할 수 있어요!

Did our talk help you feel better?
make

Are you feeling any better now after a talk?

Are you feeling better since you talked with me?

Now that we talked (it out), + *
* How do you feel?
* Do you feel better?
* Are you feeling better?
* Are you in a better mood?

어떻게 해주면 기분이 좋아지려나?

시온맘's Pick

"Is there anything I can do to make you feel better?"

다양하게 표현할 수 있어요!

How can I help you feel better?
make

What can I do to help you feel better?
make

I wonder what I can do to help you feel better.
make

Is there anything I can do to help you feel better?
make

Can you tell me what I can do to help you feel better?
make

스스로 할 수 있겠어?

시온맘's Pick

"Are you able to do it by yourself?"

다양하게 표현할 수 있어요!

Can you do it yourself?
Could by yourself?
on your own?

Are you able to do it yourself?
by yourself?
on your own?

Are you sure you do it yourself?
by yourself?
on your own?

Do you think you can do it yourself?
could by yourself?
on your own?

어떻게 하고 싶은지 이야기해줄래?

시온맘's Pick

"How would you deal with this?"

다양하게 표현할 수 있어요!

What's on your mind?

What would you like to say?

How would you deal with it?
this?

What do you want to do with it?
this?

What would you like to do with it?
this?

Can you tell me what you want to do?
let me know

Can you tell me what you (would) like to do with it?
let me know want this?

어떻게 하고 싶은지 이야기 해보렴

시온맘's Pick

"Tell me what's on your mind."

다양하게 표현할 수 있어요!

(+ Please)

Tell me what's on your mind.
Tell me what you want to do.
Tell me what you would like to say.
Tell me how you would deal with it.
this.

Tell me what you'd like to do with it.
this.

Tell me what you (would) like to do with it.
want this.

시온맘's Pick

"Let me hear what's on your mind."

이렇게도 표현할 수 있어요!

(Let me hear -)

(Let me know -)

Tell me what's on your mind.

Tell me what you want to do.

Tell me what you would like to say.

Tell me how you would deal with it.

this.

Tell me what you'd like to do with it.

this.

Tell me what you (would) like to do with it.

want this.

그렇게 해도 괜찮겠니?

시온맘's Pick

"Would this be okay for you?"

다양하게 표현할 수 있어요!

Is it okay ?
this
that

Is it okay for you?
this with
that

Are you okay with it?
this
that?

Would it be okay for you?
this with
that

너의 생각을 말해보렴

시온맘's Pick

"Please tell me what you think about this."

다양하게 표현할 수 있어요!

(+ Please)

Tell me your thoughts.

Tell me what you think.

Tell me how you feel about it.

Tell me what you think about this.

시온맘's Pick

"Let me hear what you think about this."

이렇게도 표현할 수 있어요!

(Let me hear -)

(Let me know -)

(I want to know -)

Tell me your thoughts.

(Just say -)

(Let me hear -)

(Let me know -)

(I want to know -)

Tell me what you think.

Tell me how you feel about it.

Tell me what you think about this.

너는 어떻게 생각하니?

시온맘's Pick

"What are your thoughts on that?"

다양하게 표현할 수 있어요!

What do you say?
think?

What are your thoughts?

What do you think of it?
this?
that?

How do you feel about it?
this?
that?

What do you think about it?
this?
that?

What are your thoughts on it?
this?
that?

What are your thoughts about it?
this?
that?

엄마가 어떻게 해야 하니?

시온맘's Pick

"What am I supposed to do?"

다양하게 표현할 수 있어요!

What should I do?
What can I do (for you)?
What can I help you with?
What can I do to help you?
What am I supposed to do?
What do you want me to do (for you)?

무엇을 잘못했는지 생각해보렴
네가 한 행동에 대해 생각해보렴

시온맘's Pick

"Think about your own actions."

다양하게 표현할 수 있어요!

Think about your own actions.
Think about what you did (wrong).
Think about what you've done (wrong).

시온맘's Pick

"You should think about your own actions."

이렇게도 표현할 수 있어요!

You should think about your own actions.
You should think about what you did (wrong).
You should think about what you've done (wrong).

왜 그렇게 행동한 거야?

시온맘's Pick

"What made you act in such a way?"

다양하게 표현할 수 있어요!

Why did you do that?
What made you do that?

Why did you act like that?
act that way?
act in such a way?

What made you act like that?
act that way?
act in such a way?

Why did you behave like that?
behave that way?
behave in such a way?

What made you behave like that?
behave that way?
behave in such a way?

Can you tell me why you did that?
Could

Can you tell me how that happened?
Could why

Can you tell me what made you do that?
Could

Can you tell me why you acted like that?
Could acted that way?
acted in such a way?

Can you tell me what made you act like that?
Could act that way?
act in such a way?

Can you tell me why you behaved like that?
Could behaved that way?
behaved in such a way?

Can you tell me what made you behave like that?
Could behave that way?
behave in such a way?

지금 네가 해야 할 일이니?

시온맘's Pick

"Are you supposed to be doing that right now?"

다양하게 표현할 수 있어요!

Is this what you need to do (right) now?
that

Is this what you should be doing (right) now?
that

Is this what you are supposed to do (right) now?
that / be doing

Are you supposed to do this (right) now?
that

Are you supposed to be doing this (right) now?
that

더 하고 싶은 거니?
계속 하고 싶은 거야?

시온맘's Pick

"Do you want to keep going that?"

다양하게 표현할 수 있어요!

Do you want to go on?

Do you want to do it again?
this
that

Do you want to keep doing it?
this?
that?

Do you want to continue to do it?
this?
that?

Do you want to keep going (with) it?
this?
that?

Do you want to continue (with it)?
(with this)?
(with that)?

무엇을 잘못했지?
잘못한 게 뭔지 아니?

시온맘's Pick

"Do you know what you should be sorry about?"

다양하게 표현할 수 있어요!

What did you do wrong?

What are you sorry for?
about?

Do you know your mistake?
Do you know what you did wrong?

Do you know what you should be sorry for?
about?

무엇을 잘못했는지 네가 이야기해보겠니?

시온맘's Pick

"Could you tell me what you should be sorry about?"

다양하게 표현할 수 있어요!

Can you tell me what you did wrong?
Could

Can you tell me what mistakes you made?
Could

Can you tell me what you are sorry about?
Could for?

Can you tell me what you should be sorry about?
Could for?

잘 아는 것 같구나

시온맘's Pick

"You are aware of that."

다양하게 표현할 수 있어요!

You are (well) aware of it.
that.

You (seem to) know it (very well).
that

다음엔 그런 상황에서 뭐라고 / 어떻게 이야기하면 더 좋을까?

시온맘's Pick

"If the same thing happens next time, what can you do differently?"

다양하게 표현할 수 있어요!

How can you speak differently next time?
say it

What can you say next time if this happens again?

If the same thing happens (again), how can you speak differently?
(next time), say it

If the same thing happens (again), what can you do differently?
(next time),

이럴 땐 엄마한테 뭐라고 해야 할까?

시온맘's Pick

"When this happens again, what should you say to mommy?"

★ 다양하게 표현할 수 있어요!

* 엄마가 아이에게 자신을 표현하는 경우, 문장의 목적어로 Me, Mom보다는 Mommy를 더 많이 사용합니다. 더 친근한 느낌을 담고 있기 때문입니다.

When this happens again, what can you tell me?
should mommy?

When this happens again, what can you say to me?
should mommy?

시온맘's Pick

"In this type of situation, what should you say to mommy?"

★ 이렇게도 표현할 수 있어요!

(Next time) (In the future) (In this type of situation)
When this happens again, what can you tell me?
should mommy?

When this happens again, what can you say to me?
should mommy?

엄마가 네 이야기를 듣지 않으면 네 기분이 어떻겠니?

시온맘's Pick

"How would you like it if mommy wasn't listening to you?"

다양하게 표현할 수 있어요!

* 엄마가 아이에게 자신을 표현하는 경우, 문장의 주어로 I, Mom보다는 Mommy를 더 많이 사용합니다. 더 친근한 느낌을 담고 있기 때문입니다.

How would you feel if I didn't listen to you?
like it / mommy

How would you feel if I wasn't listening to you?
like it / mommy

엄마가 너와의 약속을 지키지 않으면 네 기분이 어떻겠니?

시온맘's Pick

"How would you like it if mommy didn't keep her promise with you?"

다양하게 표현할 수 있어요!

* 엄마가 아이에게 자신을 표현하는 경우, 문장의 주어로 I, Mom보다는 Mommy를 더 많이 사용합니다. 더 친근한 느낌을 담고 있기 때문입니다.
* Mommy를 사용할 경우, 문장 안에서 my promise는 her promise로 바꾸어 주세요.

How would you feel if I didn't keep my promise with you?
like it mommy her promise

How would you feel if I didn't keep the promise I made to you?
like it mommy she

* Mommy를 사용할 경우, 문장 안에서 I는 she로 바꾸어 주세요.

엄마 마음 표현하기
Expressing Mom's Feeling

엄마가 약속 못 지켜서 미안하구나

시온맘's Pick

"I apologize I couldn't keep my word."

다양하게 표현할 수 있어요!

I apologize I couldn't keep my word.
I'm (really) sorry promise.

I apologize for not being able to keep my word.
I'm (really) sorry promise.

갑자기 급한 일이 생겨서 미안하구나
엄마도 그러고 싶은데
갑자기 급한 일이 생겼구나

시온맘's Pick

"I wish I could, but something urgent has come up."

★ 다양하게 표현할 수 있어요!

(+ I'm afraid -)
(+ I wish I could, but -)
(+ I'd also like to, but -)
(+ I really want to, but -)
(+ I'm really sorry, but -)
(+ I'd also want to, but -)
(+ I'm sorry to say this, but -)
Something urgent came up.
has come.

Something urgent (has) happened.

미안해, 엄마가 조금만 이따가 놀아줄게

시온맘's Pick

"I'm sorry. I'll have to play with you in a little while."

다양하게 표현할 수 있어요!

Sorry. I can play with you later.
I'm sorry. will a little later.
in a little while.

Sorry. I'll have to play with you later.
I'm sorry. a little later.
in a little while.

Sorry. I'm going to have to play with you later.
I'm sorry. a little later.
in a little while.

엄마가 사과할게

시온맘's Pick

"I'll apologize to you."

다양하게 표현할 수 있어요!

I'm sorry.

I apologize (to you).
I'll

엄마 사과 받아 줄 수 있을까?

시온맘's Pick

"Could you accept my apology?"

다양하게 표현할 수 있어요!

Please accept my apology.

Can you (please) accept my apology?
Could

Will you (please) accept my apology?
Would

(미안해) 엄마 용서해줄래

시온맘's Pick

"Sorry. Would you please forgive me?"

다양하게 표현할 수 있어요!

(Sorry.)
(I'm sorry.)

Can you (please) forgive me?
Could

Will you (please) forgive me?
Would

엄마가 일이 많아서 정신이 없구나

시온맘's Pick

"Mommy is swamped with things to do."

다양하게 표현할 수 있어요!

Mommy is piled with work.
loaded things to do.
swamped

Mommy is (very) busy with work.
things to do.
things to get done.

Mommy has a lot of work, so it's (very) hectic today.
things to do, chaotic
things to get done,

It's (very) hectic today as Mommy has a lot on her plate.
chaotic

Mommy has a lot on her plate, so it's (very) hectic today.
chaotic

It's (very) hectic today as Mommy has a lot of work.
chaotic
things to do.
things to get done.

* 문장 속 as 자리에 대신 올 수 있는 접속사들입니다. * for * because
* Chaotic : 혼란스러운 * Hectic : 정신없이 바쁜

엄마가 오늘 좀 힘든 날이었어

시온맘's Pick

"I've had a rough day."

다양하게 표현할 수 있어요!

Today was not my day.

It was a long day for me.
tiring
rough
tough
exhausting

I've had a long day.
tiring
rough
tough
exhausting

엄마 피곤하고 기운이 없구나

시온맘's Pick

"I feel worn out and have no energy."

다양하게 표현할 수 있어요!

I'm tired.
Mommy is

I'm drained.
Mommy is

I'm pooped.
Mommy is

I'm worn out.
Mommy is

I'm exhausted.
Mommy is

I feel tired and have no energy.
drained
pooped
worn out
exhausted

* 엄마가 아이에게 자신을 표현하는 경우, 문장의 주어로 I, Mom보다는 Mommy를 더 많이 사용합니다. 더 친근한 느낌을 담고 있기 때문입니다.
* Pooped : 녹초가 된
* Drained : 진이 빠진
* Worn out : 매우 지친
* Exhausted : 기진맥진한

그렇게 말해줘서 고맙구나

시온맘's Pick

"Thank you for saying that. That means a lot."

다양하게 표현할 수 있어요!

Thanks for saying that. + *

Thank you (so much) for saying that. + *
(very much)

I would like to thank you (so much) for saying that. + *

* That means a lot.
* I really appreciate it.

너의 마음을 말해줘서 고맙구나

시온맘's Pick

"Thank you for telling me about how you feel. That means a lot."

다양하게 표현할 수 있어요!

Thank you (so much) for saying that. + *

Thank you (so much) for telling me (about it). + *
(about how you feel).

Thank you (so much) for sharing (how you feel). + *
telling me
letting me know

* That means a lot.
* I really appreciate it.

너의 생각을 말해줘서 고맙구나

시온맘's Pick

"Thank you for telling me what's on your mind. That means a lot."

다양하게 표현할 수 있어요!

Thank you (so much) for saying that. + *

Thank you (so much) for telling me what you think. + *
what's on your mind.

Thank you (so much) for sharing your thoughts with me. + *

Thank you (so much) for letting me know what you think. + *
what's on your mind.

* That means a lot.
* I really appreciate it.

엄마 말 잘 따라줘서 고마워

시온맘's Pick

"Thank you very much for behaving so well and listening to mommy."

다양하게 표현할 수 있어요!

* 엄마가 아이에게 자신을 표현하는 경우, 문장의 목적어로 Me, Mom보다는 Mommy를 더 많이 사용합니다. 더 친근한 느낌을 담고 있기 때문입니다.

Thanks for listening.

Thank you (so much) for listening (to me).
(very much) (to mommy).

Thank you (so much) for behaving so well and listening to me.
(very much) mommy.

말 잘 들어서 이쁘구나

시온맘's Pick

"You are so well-behaved."

다양하게 표현할 수 있어요!

* 엄마가 아이에게 자신을 표현하는 경우, 문장의 목적어로 Me, Mom보다는 Mommy를 더 많이 사용합니다. 더 친근한 느낌을 담고 있기 때문입니다.

You are so well-behaved.

You are behaving so well.

You are showing good behavior.

You are doing a good job listening to me.
great mommy.

이해해줘서 고맙구나

시온맘's Pick

"Thank you for being so understanding."

다양하게 표현할 수 있어요!

* 엄마가 아이에게 자신을 표현하는 경우, 문장의 목적어로 Me, Mom보다는 Mommy를 더 많이 사용합니다. 더 친근한 느낌을 담고 있기 때문입니다.

Thank you for understanding me.
mommy.

Thank you for (your) understanding.

Thank you for being so understanding.

다시 밝아진 모습 보니 엄마도 기분이 좋네

시온맘's Pick

"It's good that you are back to being yourself."

다양하게 표현할 수 있어요!

I'm glad to see you smiling again.
It's good
I'm happy

I'm glad that you are happy again.
It's good
I'm happy

I'm glad to see you being happy again.
It's good
I'm happy

I'm glad to see that smile on your face (again).
It's good
I'm happy

I'm glad that you are back to being happy (again).
It's good normal
I'm happy yourself

엄마가 너를 (얼마나) 사랑하는지 알지

시온맘's Pick

"Do you know I adore you?"

다양하게 표현할 수 있어요!

Do you know (how much) I love you?
adore
care for

You know (how much) I love you, right?
adore
care for

엄마와의 약속을 지키지 않으면, 엄마도 약속대로 안 해줄 거야

시온맘's Pick

"Unless you keep your word, I won't either."

다양하게 표현할 수 있어요!

If you break your word, I will, too.
promise,

Unless you keep your word, I won't (keep mine) either.
promise,

If you don't keep your word, I won't (keep mine) either.
promise,

If you don't keep the promise you made with me, I won't (keep mine) either.

말 잘 듣는다고 약속했지, 그렇지?

시온맘's Pick

"You promised you would listen to mommy, right?"

다양하게 표현할 수 있어요!

You promised (that) you would behave, right?
listen to mommy,

네가 버릇없게 굴면 엄마는 속상해
네가 그러면 엄마 마음이 아프단다
네가 그렇게 행동할 때마다
엄마 마음이 슬프단다 / 아프단다

시온맘's Pick

"If you act in such a way, it saddens me."

다양하게 표현할 수 있어요!

If you act like that, it saddens me.
act that way,
act in such a way,

If you act like that, it makes me sad.
act that way,
act in such a way,

If you misbehave, it saddens me.
behave like that,
behave that way,
behave in such a way,

If you misbehave, it makes me sad.
behave like that,
behave that way,
behave in such a way,

It hurts mom's feelings when you act like that.
act that way.
act in such a way.

It hurts mom's feelings when you misbehave.
behave like that.
behave that way.
behave in such a way.

I feel sad whenever you act like that.
each time act that way.
every time act in such a way.

I feel sad whenever you misbehave.
each time behave like that.
every time behave that way.
behave in such a way.

또 그러면 엄마가 정말 속상할 거야

시온맘's Pick

"I would be upset if you behave that way."

다양하게 표현할 수 있어요!

I will be sad if this happens again.
would mad
upset

I will feel sad if this happens again.
would mad
upset

I will not be happy if this happens again.
would

I will not be happy to see this happen again.
would

I will be sad if you misbehave. (again).
would mad behave like that.
upset behave that way.
behave in such a way.

I will feel sad if you misbehave. (again).
would mad behave like that.
upset behave that way.
behave in such a way.

I will be sad if you act like that. (again).
would mad act that way.
upset act in such a way.

I will feel sad if you act like that. (again).
would mad act that way.
upset act in such a way.

If you misbehave (again), it will make me sad.
behave like that mad.
behave that way upset.
behave in such a way

If you act like that (again), it will make me sad.
act that way mad.
act in such away upset.

다신 그러지 말자

시온맘's Pick

"Don't ever do that again."

다양하게 표현할 수 있어요!

(+ Please)

Don't let this happen again.

Don't (ever) do it again.
that

(+ Please 안 됨)

I hope it does not happen again.

다신 그러지 않았으면 해

시온맘's Pick

"I'd like it if you didn't behave in such a way."

다양하게 표현할 수 있어요!

I hope you won't act like that (again).
act that way
act in such a way

I hope you wouldn't act like that (again).
act that way
act in such a way

I hope you won't misbehave (again).
behave like that
behave that way
behave in such a way

I hope you wouldn't misbehave (again).
behave like that
behave that way
behave in such a way

I don't want you to act like that (again).
act that way
act in such a way

I don't want you to misbehave (again).
behave like that
behave that way
behave in such a way

I'd like it if you didn't act like that (again).
act that way
act in such a way

I'd like it if you didn't misbehave (again).
behave like that
behave that way
behave in such a way

잘 안 될 땐 짜증내지 말고, "엄마! 도와주세요!"라고 이야기 해주면 좋겠어. 알겠지?

시온맘's Pick

"If you are having trouble, ask for help instead of throwing a fit. Okay?"

다양하게 표현할 수 있어요!

If you are having trouble, ask for help instead of yelling at me. Okay?
throwing a fit.
getting annoyed.

If you need help, I'd like for you to say, "Help, mommy!" instead of
yelling at me.
throwing a fit.
getting annoyed.

Don't yell at me when you are having trouble. Instead, (you can) ask for help.
throw a fit / in need of help. / (you should)
get annoyed

Don't yell at me when you are having trouble. Instead, (you can) say, "Help, mommy!"
throw a fit / in need of help. / (you should)
get annoyed

울지 말고 이야기했으면 좋겠어

시온맘's Pick

"Don't cry, instead talk to me."

다양하게 표현할 수 있어요!

Don't cry, (instead) talk to me.

I'd like (for) you to stop crying and talk to me instead.
use your words

시온맘's Pick

"I don't want you to cry, instead talk to me."

이렇게도 표현할 수 있어요!

I don't want you to cry, (instead) talk to me.

말로 하렴

시온맘's Pick

"Say it in clear words."

다양하게 표현할 수 있어요!

(+ Please)
Speak clearly.
Say it

Use your words.
clear

Speak in clear words.
Say it

Say what you want (to say) clearly.
Tell me in clear words.
in a way I can understand you.
in a way I could understand you.
in the way I can understand you.

시온맘's Pick

"I'd like for you to **say it in clear words.**"

이렇게도 표현할 수 있어요!

(+ I want you to -)
(+ I'd like (for) you to -)

Speak clearly.
Say it

Use your words.
clear

Speak in clear words.
Say it

Say what you want (to say) clearly.
Tell me in clear words.
in the way I could understand you.

양해 구하기

Seeking Understanding

엄마 잠깐만 쉬게 혼자 놀아 볼래

시온맘's Pick

"Mommy needs some time to rest. Could you play on your own for a little while?"

다양하게 표현할 수 있어요!

* Mommy needs some (time to) rest.

* + Can you play alone for a bit?
  Will by yourself
  Could on your own
  Would

* + Can you play alone so that I can rest for a bit?
  Will by yourself
  Could on your own
  Would

* + Can you give mommy a break and play alone for a bit?
  Will a little break
  Could some time
  Would

* + Can you give mommy a break and play by yourself for a bit?
  Will a little break
  Could some time
  Would

* + Can you give mommy a break and play on your own for a bit?
    Will a little break
    Could some time
    Would

* for a bit 자리를 대신할 수 있는 표현들입니다.

* for a minute
* for a second
* for a moment
* for a short time
* for a little while
* for a (little) bit

아빠한테 같이 놀아달라고 해볼래?

시온맘's Pick

"Why don't you go and ask Daddy if he could play with you?"

다양하게 표현할 수 있어요!

Why don't you ask Daddy to play with you?

Why don't you go and ask Daddy if he can play with you?
could

아빠 피곤하신가봐, 쉬시게 하자

시온맘's Pick

"Daddy seems tired. Give him some time to take a break."

다양하게 표현할 수 있어요!

* Daddy looks tired.
  seems
  must be

* + Let him rest.

* + Leave him alone.

* + Give him a break.

* + Let him take a rest.
  break.

* + Daddy needs some rest.

* + Give him some time to rest.

* + Give him some time to take a rest.
  break.

시온맘's Pick

"Daddy seems tired. You should give him some time to take a break."

이렇게도 표현할 수 있어요!

* Daddy looks tired.
  seems
  must be

* + We should let him rest.
  You should

* + We should leave him alone.
  You should

* + We should give him a break.
  You should

* + We should let him take a rest.
  You should break.

* + We should give him some time to rest.
  You should

* + We should give him some time to take a rest.
  You should break.

엄마가 설거지 다하고 놀아줘도 될까?

시온맘's Pick

"I'll have playtime after I'm finished with the dishes. Would that be okay with you?"

다양하게 표현할 수 있어요!

* Is that okay with you?

* Can I play with you then?
  Could

* Will that be okay with you?
  Would

I'll have playtime after finishing the dishes. + *
I finish
I'm done with
I'm finished with

I'll have the time to play with you after finishing the dishes. + *
I finish
I'm done with
I'm finished with

Is it okay if I play with you once I finish (washing) the dishes?

Is it okay if I play with you after I'm done with (washing) the dishes?
finished

시온맘's Pick

"Will it be okay if I play with you once I finish the dishes?"

이렇게도 표현할 수 있어요!

(Will it be okay if - ?)
(Would it be okay if - ?)
Is it okay if I play with you once I finish (washing) the dishes?

Is it okay if I play with you after I'm done with (washing) the dishes?
finished

엄마가 빨래 다하고 놀아줘도 될까?

시온맘's Pick

"I'll have the time to play with you after I'm done with the laundry. Could I play with you then?"

다양하게 표현할 수 있어요!

* Is that okay with you?

* Will that be okay with you?
  Would

* Can I play with you then?
  Could

I'll have playtime after finishing the laundry. + *
I finish
I'm done with
I'm finished with

I'll have the time to play with you after finishing the laundry. + *
I finish
I'm done with
I'm finished with

Is it okay if I play with you once I finish (doing) the laundry?

Is it okay if I play with you after I'm done with (the) laundry?
finished

시온맘's Pick

"Would it be okay if I play with you after I'm finished with laundry?"

이렇게도 표현할 수 있어요!

(Will it be okay if - ?)
(Would it be okay if - ?)
Is it okay if I play with you once I finish (doing) the laundry?

Is it okay if I play with you after I'm done with (the) laundry?
finished

엄마가 집 청소 다하고 놀아줘도 될까?

시온맘's Pick

"I'll have the time to play with you after I finish the clean-up. Could I play with you then?"

다양하게 표현할 수 있어요!

* Is that okay with you?

* Will that be okay with you?
  Would

* Can I play with you then?
  Could

I'll have playtime after finishing the clean-up. + *
I finish
I'm done with
I'm finished with

I'll have playtime after finishing cleaning (the house). + *
I finish
I'm done with
I'm finished with

I'll have the time to play with you after finishing the clean-up. + *
I finish
I'm done with
I'm finished with

I'll have the time to play with you after finishing cleaning (the house). + *
I finish
I'm done with
I'm finished with

Is it okay if I play with you once I finish cleaning?
the clean-up?
cleaning the house?

Is it okay if I play with you after I'm done with cleaning?
finished the clean-up?
cleaning the house?

시온맘's Pick

"Will it be okay if I play with you after I'm finished with the clean-up?"

이렇게도 표현할 수 있어요!

(Will it be okay if - ?)
(Would it be okay if - ?)
Is it okay if I play with you once I finish cleaning?
the clean-up?
cleaning the house?

Is it okay if I play with you after I'm done with cleaning?
finished the clean-up?
cleaning the house?

거의 다했어

시온맘's Pick

"I'm pretty much finished."

다양하게 표현할 수 있어요!

I will be done soon.
finished

(I'm) Almost done.
there.
finished.

(I'm) Pretty much done.
finished.

* soon 자리에 대신 사용할 수 있는 표현들입니다.

* shortly
* in a few
* in a little bit
* in a moment
* in a little while

이것만 하면 끝나

시온맘's Pick

"This is all I have left."

다양하게 표현할 수 있어요!

I'll be done after this.
finished

This is all I have left (to do).

Once I get this (part) done, I'll be done.
finished.

헹구기만 하면 돼

시온맘's Pick

"I only have rinsing out the dishes left. Once I get this part done, I'll be finished."

다양하게 표현할 수 있어요!

* I'll be done after this.
  finished

* This is all I have left (to do).

* Once I get this (part) done, I'll be done.
  finished.

I'm rinsing them (out). + *
the dishes

I just have to rinse them (out). + *
only

I just have rinsing (out the dishes) left (to do). + *
only

The only thing I have left (to do) is rinsing (out) the dishes. + *
to rinse

(빨래) 널기만 하면 돼

시온맘's Pick

"The only thing I have left is hanging out the laundry.
This is all I have left to do."

다양하게 표현할 수 있어요!

* This is all I have left (to do).

* I'll be done after this.
finished

* Once I get this (part) done, I'll be done.
finished.

I'm hanging them (out). + *
the laundry

I just have to hang them (out). + *
only the laundry

I just have hanging (out the laundry) left (to do). + *
only

The only thing I have left (to do) is to hang (out) the laundry. + *
hanging

(빨래) 개고 수납만 하면 돼

시온맘's Pick

"The only thing I have left is folding and putting the laundry in the drawer. I'll be done after this."

다양하게 표현할 수 있어요!

* This is all I have left (to do).

* I'll be done after this.
  finished

* Once I get this (part) done, I'll be done.
  finished.

I'm folding them and will put them in the drawer. + *
the laundry

I just have to fold them and put them in the drawer. + *
only / the laundry

I just have folding and putting them in the drawer left (to do). + *
only / the laundry

The only thing I have left (to do) is to fold and put them in the drawer. + *
the laundry

The only thing I have left (to do) is folding and putting them in the drawer. + *
the laundry

청소기만 돌리면 돼

시온맘's Pick

"I'm vacuuming the floor. This is all I have left to do."

다양하게 표현할 수 있어요!

* This is all I have left (to do).

* I'll be done after this.
  finished

* Once I get this (part) done, I'll be done.
  finished.

I'm vacuuming the floor. + *

I just have to vacuum the floor. + *
only

I just have vacuuming (the floor) left (to do). + *
only

The only thing I have left (to do) is to vacuum the floor. + *
vacuuming

걸레질만 하면 돼

시온맘's Pick

"The only thing I have left to do is to wipe the floor.
Once I get this part done, I'll be finished."

다양하게 표현할 수 있어요!

* This is all I have left (to do).

* I'll be done after this.
finished

* Once I get this (part) done, I'll be done.
finished.

I'm wiping the floor. + *

I just have to wipe the floor + *
only

I just have wiping (the floor) left (to do). + *
only

The only thing I have left (to do) is wiping the floor. + *
to wipe

* 손걸레질을 하다 Wipe
* 대걸레질을 하다 Mop

엄마 여기 잠깐 누워 있어도 될까

시온맘's Pick

"Will it be okay for me to lie down here for a little while?"

다양하게 표현할 수 있어요!

(+ Please)
(Can I - ?)
(Could I - ?)
(Is it okay if I - ?)
(Will it be okay if I - ?)
(Would it be okay if I - ?)
(Will it be okay for me to - ?)
(Would it be okay for me to - ?)

Let me lie down here for a bit.

* for a bit 자리를 대신할 수 있는 표현들입니다.

* for a minute
* for a second
* for a moment
* for a (little) bit
* for a short time
* for a little while

엄마 좀 쉬어도 될까

시온맘's Pick

"Will it be okay if I have a rest here for a bit?"

다양하게 표현할 수 있어요!

(+ Please)
(Can I - ?)
(Could I - ?)
(Is it okay if I - ?)
(Will it be okay if I - ?)
(Would it be okay if I - ?)
(Will it be okay for me to - ?)
(Would it be okay for me to - ?)

Let me rest here for a bit.
relax
take a rest
have a rest
take a break
get some rest

* for a bit 자리를 대신할 수 있는 표현들입니다.
* for a minute
* for a second
* for a moment
* for a (little) bit
* for a short time
* for a little while

제3의 대안 제시하기

A Third Alternative

너무 부담 갖지 마렴
너무 스트레스 받지 마렴

시온맘's Pick

"Please don't get stressed out."

다양하게 표현할 수 있어요!

(+ Please)
Don't stress (too much).

Don't be (too) pressured.
get overwhelmed.
feel

Don't be (too) stressed (out).
get
feel

Don't be (too) stressed about it.
get
feel

Don't stress yourself out (too much).

시온맘's Pick

"Please, I don't want you to get stressed out."

이렇게도 표현할 수 있어요!

* I don't로 시작하는 문장에서 Please, 다음과 같이 Please 뒤에 콤마(,)를 붙여 사용해야 합니다.

(+ Please,)

I don't want you to be (too) stressed (out).
get
feel

I don't want you to be (too) stressed about it.
get
feel

I don't want you to be (too) pressured.
get overwhelmed.
feel

I don't want you to be (too) pressured about it.
get overwhelmed.
feel

괜찮아, 하기 싫으면 안 해도 된단다

시온맘's Pick

"It's okay. If you don't want to do it, you don't have to."

별거 아닌 일로 속 태우지 마렴

시온맘's Pick

"Don't let little things get to you."

다양하게 표현할 수 있어요!

(+ Please)

Don't sweat (on) the small stuff.
Don't let (the) little things get to you.

할 수 있는 만큼만 해보렴

시온맘's Pick

"Do it as best as you could."

다양하게 표현할 수 있어요!

Do it as best as you can.
could.

Do it as long as you can.
could.

Do it as much as you can.
could.

Do it as much as you'd like to (do).

Do it as much as you are able to (do).

Do as much as you feel like doing.
You can do as much as you feel like doing.

시온맘's Pick

"You can do it as best as you could."

이렇게도 표현할 수 있어요!

You can do it as best as you can.
could.

You can do it as long as you can.
could.

You can do (it) as much as you can.
could.

You can do (it) as much as you'd like to (do).

You can do (it) as much as you are able to (do).

도움이 필요하면 말해

시온맘's Pick

"Tell me if you are in need of help."

다양하게 표현할 수 있어요!

Tell me if you need (my) help.

Tell me if you are in need of help.

시온맘's Pick

"You can tell me if you are in need of help."

이렇게도 표현할 수 있어요!

You can tell me if you need (my) help.

You can tell me if you are in need of help.

시온맘's Pick

"Let me know if you are in need of help."

이렇게도 표현할 수 있어요!

Let me know if you need (my) help.

Let me know if you are in need of help.

엄마가 도와줄게

시온맘's Pick

"Let me help you take care of it."

다양하게 표현할 수 있어요!

I'll help you (out).
I can
Let me

I'll give you a hand.
I can
Let me

I'll (help you) take care of it.
I can
Let me

(지금은 엄마가 도와줄게)
그 다음부턴 혼자 잘할 수 있을 거야

시온맘's Pick

"Mommy will help you this time. Next time, you can do a lot better."

다양하게 표현할 수 있어요!

* 엄마가 아이에게 자신을 표현하는 경우, 문장의 주어로 I, Mom보다는 Mommy를 더 많이 사용합니다. 더 친근한 느낌을 담고 있기 때문입니다.

* (I will help you this time.)
  Mommy

* (This time, I will help you.)
  Mommy

* + Then, you can do it better (than before / now).
  Next time, will

* + Then, you can do a lot better (than before / now).
  Next time, will much

* + Then, you can be great (when you are) on your own.
  Next time, will
  will be able to

* + Then, you can be better (when you are) on your own.
Next time will
will be able to

* + Then, you can do great (when you are) on your own.
Next time will
will be able to

* + Then, you can do (it) better (when you are) on your own.
Next time will
will be able to

* + Then, you can do a good job (when you are) on your own.
Next time, will
will be able to

* + Then, you can do a great job (when you are) on your own.
Next time, will
will be able to

우리 뭐하고 놀까?
뭐하고 놀면 좋을까?

시온맘's Pick

"What kind of game do you want to play?"

다양하게 표현할 수 있어요!

What shall we do (to have fun)?
should we
do you want to
would you like to

What kind of game will be good?
do you want to play?

무엇을 하면 좋을까?

시온맘's Pick

"What would you like to do?"

다양하게 표현할 수 있어요!

What do you like to do?
would

아빠한테 같이 놀아달라고 해볼래?

시온맘's Pick

"Why don't you go and ask Daddy if he could play with you?"

다양하게 표현할 수 있어요!

Why don't you ask Daddy to play with you?

Why don't you go and ask Daddy if he can play with you?
could

같이 놀 사람?

시온맘's Pick

"Does anyone want to play with me?"

다양하게 표현할 수 있어요!

Who wants to play (with me)?

Does anyone want to play (with me)?

같이 한 번 생각해보자

시온맘's Pick

"If you and I put our thoughts together, we can figure that out."

다양하게 표현할 수 있어요!

Let's think about it together.
We should think about it together.
Why don't we think about it together?

If we think together, we could figure it out.
you and I / this / that

If we put our thoughts together, we can figure it out.
you and I / this / that

같이 한 번 해결해보자

시온맘's Pick

"Let's get that sorted right together."

다양하게 표현할 수 있어요!

Let's sort it out together.
this
that

Let's figure it out together.
this
that

Let's get it sorted (right) together.
this
that

시온맘's Pick

"We should **get that sorted right together.**"

이렇게도 표현할 수 있어요!

(We should -)
(Why don't we - ?)
Let's sort it out together.
this
that

Let's figure it out together.
this
that

Let's get it sorted (right) together.
this
that

이것도 / 그것도 싫어?

시온맘's Pick

"This doesn't pique your interest?"

다양하게 표현할 수 있어요!

Is this not "it" ?

You don't like that, either?
want

You don't like any of these?
want

This isn't what you wanted?

None of these fit your taste?

This doesn't pique your interest?

* Pique one's interest : ~의 관심을 끌다

이렇게 해보는 건 어떨까?

시온맘's Pick

"What about, you try doing it this way?"

다양하게 표현할 수 있어요!

Maybe you can do it like this.
try this way.

* 위 문장에서 can 자리에 대신 올 수 있는 조동사들입니다.

* could
* should

Why don't you do it like this?
try this way?
try doing

How about, you do it like this?
What try this way?
try doing

이렇게 해보면 좋겠다

시온맘's Pick

"It would be great if you could do it this way."

다양하게 표현할 수 있어요!

It would be nice if you could do it like this.
great / this way.

It would be nice if you could try (doing) it like this.
great / this way.

다른 걸 더 잘하잖아, 잘하는 걸 해볼까?

시온맘's Pick

"There are other things you are better at. Why don't we try those?"

다양하게 표현할 수 있어요!

There are other things you are better at. Should we try those?
Why don't

You are better at other things. Do you want to do something that you're good at (instead)?

단 거 먹으면 기운이 좀 날 거야

시온맘's Pick

"Having sweets will put you in a better mood."

다양하게 표현할 수 있어요!

Sweets will pick you up.
Something sweet

Eating sweets will pick you up.
something sweet

Having sweets will pick you up.
something sweet

Sweets will make you feel better.
Something sweet

Eating sweets will make you feel better.
something sweet

Having sweets will make you feel better.
something sweet

Sweets will put you in a good mood.
Something sweet better

Eating sweets will put you in a good mood.
something sweet better

Having sweets will put you in a good mood.
something sweet better

It'll make you feel better if you eat some sweets.
have

화 풀어, 엄마가 놀아줄게

시온맘's Pick

"Don't be so mad at me. I'll play with you."

다양하게 표현할 수 있어요!

(+ Come on.)
Forgive me. I'll play with you.

Don't be so sad (at me). I'll play with you.
mad
upset
angry

업혀 보렴
엄마가 업어 줄게

시온맘's Pick

"Let me carry you on my back."

다양하게 표현할 수 있어요!

Get on my back.

I'll carry you on my back.
Let me

I'll give you a piggyback ride.
Let me

엄마랑 어떤 놀이하고 싶어?

시온맘's Pick

"What activity would you like to do with mommy?"

다양하게 표현할 수 있어요!

* 엄마가 아이에게 자신을 표현하는 경우, 문장의 목적어로 Me, Mom보다는 Mommy를 더 많이 사용합니다. 더 친근한 느낌을 담고 있기 때문입니다.

What do you like to do (the most) with me?
want / mommy?

What would you like to do (the most) with me?
mommy?

What toy do you like to do with me (the most)?
game / want / mommy
activity

What toy would you like to do with me (the most)?
game / mommy
activity

이거 갖고 놀래?
이거 가지고 놀까?

시온맘's Pick

"Would you want to play with this?"

다양하게 표현할 수 있어요!

Should we play with this?

Do you want to play with this?

Would you like to play with this?
want

그림 그릴래?
그림 그릴까?

시온맘's Pick

"Should we draw a picture?"

다양하게 표현할 수 있어요!

Should we draw (a picture)?

Do you want to draw (a picture)?

Would you like to draw (a picture)?
want

엄마가 크레파스 가져올게

시온맘's Pick

"Let me go get crayons."

다양하게 표현할 수 있어요!

I'll go get crayons.
Let me grab

종이접기 할까?
종이접기 하고 싶니?

시온맘's Pick

"Do you want to do origami?"

다양하게 표현할 수 있어요!

Should we do origami?

Do you want to do origami?

Would you like to do origami?
want

소꿉놀이 할까?
소꿉놀이 하고 싶니?

시온맘's Pick

"Would you like to play grown-up?"

다양하게 표현할 수 있어요!

Should we play house?
grown-up?

Do you want to play house?
grown-up?

Would you like to play house?
want grown-up?

찰흙놀이 할까?
찰흙놀이 하고 싶니?

시온맘's Pick

"Should we play with clay?"

다양하게 표현할 수 있어요!

Should we play with clay?

Do you want to play with clay?

Would you like to play with clay?
want

우리 오늘 하루 종일 집에만 있었네

시온맘's Pick

"We've stayed inside all day."

다양하게 표현할 수 있어요!

We've stayed inside all day (long).
at home

엄마랑 산책 나갈까?

시온맘's Pick

"Do you want to have a stroll?"

다양하게 표현할 수 있어요!

Do you want to walk?

Do you want to take a walk?
a stroll?

Do you want to have a walk?
a stroll?

Do you want to go for a walk?
a stroll?

시온맘's Pick

"Would you like to **have a stroll?**"

이렇게도 표현할 수 있어요!

Would you like to **walk?**

Would you like to **take** a walk?
a stroll?

Would you like to **have** a walk?
a stroll?

Would you like to **go for** a walk?
a stroll?

나가서 바람 쐬고 오자

시온맘's Pick

"Let's step outside to get some fresh air."

다양하게 표현할 수 있어요!

Let's (go) get some fresh air.

Let's step out to get some fresh air.
outside

Let's step out and get some fresh air.
outside

시온맘's Pick

"Why don't we step outside to get some fresh air?"

이렇게도 표현할 수 있어요!

Why don't we (go) get some fresh air?

Why don't we step out to get some fresh air?
outside

Why don't we step out and get some fresh air?
outside

나가서 잠깐 바람 좀 쐬고 오자

시온맘's Pick

"Let's step outside real quick for some fresh air."

다양하게 표현할 수 있어요!

Let's go out real quick for some fresh air.
outside to get

Let's step out real quick for some fresh air.
outside to get

Let's (go) get some fresh air for a minute.

Let's go out for a minute to get some fresh air.
outside and

Let's step out for a minute to get some fresh air.
outside and

시온맘's Pick

"Why don't we step outside real quick for some fresh air?"

이렇게도 표현할 수 있어요!

Why don't we go out real quick for some fresh air?
outside to get

Why don't we step out real quick for some fresh air?
outside to get

Why don't we (go) get some fresh air for a minute?

Why don't we go out for a minute to get some fresh air?
outside and

Why don't we step out for a minute to get some fresh air?
outside and

밖에 나가서 놀래?
밖에 나가서 놀고 싶니?

시온맘's Pick

"Would you want to play outdoors?"

다양하게 표현할 수 있어요!

Should we play outside?
outdoors?

Do you want to play outside?
outdoors?

Would you like to play outside?
want outdoors?

놀이터 가서 놀래?
놀이터 가서 놀고 싶니?

시온맘's Pick

"Do you want to go play at the playground?"

다양하게 표현할 수 있어요!

Should we go play at the playground?

Do you want to go play at the playground?

Would you like to go play at the playground?
want

킥보드 탈래?
킥보드 타고 싶니?

시온맘's Pick

"Should we ride a scooter?"

다양하게 표현할 수 있어요!

Should we ride a scooter?

Do you want to ride a scooter?

Would you like to ride a scooter?
want

자전거 탈래?
자전거 타고 싶니?

시온맘's Pick

"Would you want to ride a bike?"

다양하게 표현할 수 있어요!

Should we ride a bike?

Do you want to ride a bike?

Would you like to ride a bike?
want

같이 술래잡기 하는 건 어때?

시온맘's Pick

"What about we play freeze tag?"

다양하게 표현할 수 있어요!

Let's play (freeze) tag.

Should we play (freeze) tag?

How about we play (freeze) tag?
What

Why don't we play (freeze) tag?
Do you want to

같이 숨바꼭질 하는 건 어때?

시온맘's Pick

"Should we play hide and seek?"

다양하게 표현할 수 있어요!

Let's play hide and seek.

Should we play hide and seek?

How about we play hide and seek?
What

Why don't we play hide and seek?
Do you want to

공놀이 하자!

시온맘's Pick

"Let's play throw and catch."

다양하게 표현할 수 있어요!

Let's play ball.
catch.

Let's play toss and catch.
throw

Let's play (catch) with a ball.

시온맘's Pick

"Why don't we play throw and catch?"

이렇게도 표현할 수 있어요!

Why don't we play ball?
catch?

Why don't we play toss and catch?
throw

Why don't we play (catch) with a ball?

엄마가 맛있는 거 해줄게

시온맘's Pick

"I will fix something delicious for you."

다양하게 표현할 수 있어요!

I will fix something yummy for you.
cook delicious
make

시온맘's Pick

"Let me fix something delicious for you."

이렇게도 표현할 수 있어요!

Let me fix something yummy for you.
cook delicious
make

엄마가 맛있는 거 사줄게

시온맘's Pick

"I will get something delicious for you."

다양하게 표현할 수 있어요!

I will get you something yummy.
buy / delicious

I will get something yummy for you.
buy / delicious

I will take you out to go get something yummy.
delicious.

시온맘's Pick

"Let me get something delicious for you."

이렇게도 표현할 수 있어요!

Let me get you something yummy.
buy / delicious

Let me get something yummy for you.
buy / delicious

Let me take you out to go get something yummy.
delicious.

엄마랑 같이 맛있는 거 먹으러 가자구나

시온맘's Pick

"Let's **eat out.**"

다양하게 표현할 수 있어요!

Let's eat out.

Let's go eat something yummy.
delicious.

시온맘's Pick

"Why don't we **eat out?**"

이렇게도 표현할 수 있어요!

Why don't we eat out?

Why don't we go eat something yummy?
delicious?

그럼 나가 보자

시온맘's Pick

"Let's **get going.**"

다양하게 표현할 수 있어요!

Let's go.
get going.

Let's go out.
outside.

Let's head (our way) out.

시온맘's Pick

"Why don't we **get going?**"

이렇게도 표현할 수 있어요!

Why don't we go?
get going?

Why don't we go out?
outside?

Why don't we head (our way) out?

칭찬하기
Giving Compliments

착하구나

시온맘's Pick

"You are such a nice girl."

다양하게 표현할 수 있어요!

* 딸인 경우 Girl, 아들인 경우 Boy.

How nice of you!

What a good boy.
girl.

You are such a nice boy.
girl.

That's (very) nice of you.

말을 참 예쁘게 하는구나

시온맘's Pick

"You speak in a very sweet way."

다양하게 표현할 수 있어요!

You speak in a very nice way.
kind
polite
sweet
thoughtful

이해해줘서 고맙구나

시온맘's Pick

"Thank you for being so understanding."

다양하게 표현할 수 있어요!

* 엄마가 아이에게 자신을 표현하는 경우, 문장의 목적어로 Me와 Mom보다는 Mommy를 더 많이 사용합니다. 더 친근한 느낌을 담고 있기 때문입니다.

Thank you for (your) understanding.

Thank you for being so understanding.

Thank you for understanding me.
mommy.

이해할 줄도 알고,
엄마 마음이 따뜻해지네

시온맘's Pick

"It warms my heart that you could understand other people."

다양하게 표현할 수 있어요!

* 이해 받는 상대가 여자인 경우 Her, 남자인 경우 Him.

I'm so touched to see that you are able to understand him.
her.
other people.

I'm so touched (by the fact) that you (could) understand him.
her.
other people.

It (really) warms my heart to see that you are able to understand him.
her.
other people.

It (really) warms my heart (to know) that you (could) understand him.
her.
other people.

다 컸네, 다 컸어

시온맘's Pick

"When did you become such a big girl?"

다양하게 표현할 수 있어요!

* 딸인 경우 Girl, 아들인 경우 Boy.

You're all grown now.

When did you get so big?

Look at how much you've grown.

You are (such a) big boy now.
girl

When did you grow up so big?
much?

When did you become such a big boy?
girl?

이제 다 큰 누나네!
이제 다 큰 형이네!

시온맘's Pick

“You are a big boy now.”

다양하게 표현할 수 있어요!

* 딸인 경우 Girl, 아들인 경우 Boy.

You are a big boy (now).
girl

그래준다면 정말 좋겠구나

시온맘's Pick

"That would be wonderful, if you could do that."

다양하게 표현할 수 있어요!

That would be awesome, if you could do that.
wonderful,
really great,

If you could do that, that would be awesome.
wonderful.
really great.

잘했어!

시온맘's Pick

"You did a good job."

다양하게 표현할 수 있어요!

* 딸인 경우 Girl, 아들인 경우 Boy.

Nice.

Good.

Excellent.

Great job.

Well done.

Good boy.
girl.

Two thumbs up.

You did a nice job.
good
great

최고야!

시온맘's Pick

"There's no one better than you."

다양하게 표현할 수 있어요!

Two thumbs up.

You are the best.

There's no one better than you.

점점 더 잘하는데

시온맘's Pick

"You're showing progress."

다양하게 표현할 수 있어요!

You're improving. + *
You're showing progress. + *
You're showing improvement. + *

I'm seeing progress.+ *
I'm seeing improvement. + *
I see that you're getting better at this. + *

You're getting so good at it.
You're getting better and better.
You're doing a lot better than before.

* 위 표시된 문장들 뒤에 다음 아래 표현들 중 하나를 더해주셔도 좋습니다.

* each day
* every day
* day by day

아주 좋은 질문이야

시온맘's Pick

"That's a really great question."

다양하게 표현할 수 있어요!

That's a very good question.
great

That's a really good question.
great

좋은 생각이야

시온맘's Pick

"I think that would be a wonderful idea."

다양하게 표현할 수 있어요!

Sounds good.
great.
wonderful.

That's a good idea.
great
wonderful

What a good idea.
great
wonderful

I think that would be a good idea.
great
wonderful

엄마는 네가 있어서 감사해

시온맘's Pick

"I feel grateful for you."

다양하게 표현할 수 있어요!

I am grateful for you.
feel

I am thankful for you.
feel

I am thankful to have you.
feel

I thank God for you being my child.

네 덕분에 엄마가 으쓱해

시온맘's Pick

"You mean so much to mommy."

다양하게 표현할 수 있어요!

* 엄마가 아이에게 자신을 표현하는 경우, 문장의 목적어로 Me, Mom보다는 Mommy를 더 많이 사용합니다. 더 친근한 느낌을 담고 있기 때문입니다.

You make me proud.

You mean so much to me.
mommy.

정말 용감했어
정말 씩씩했어

시온맘's Pick

"That was really brave of you."

다양하게 표현할 수 있어요!

You were very / really brave.

That was very / really brave (of you).

What you did was very / really brave.

엄마는 네가 해낼 줄 알았어

시온맘's Pick

"I knew you would get the hang of it."

다양하게 표현할 수 있어요!

I knew you could do it.

I knew you would make it.

I knew you'd be able to do it.

I knew you could go through it.
would

I knew you would get the hang of it.

말 예쁘게 잘했어

시온맘's Pick

"It's nice of you to speak in a very sweet way. Well done!"

다양하게 표현할 수 있어요!

You spoke very nicely.
politely.

It's nice of you to speak in a very nice way.
kind
polite
sweet
thoughtful

* 위 문장들 전이나 후에 다음 아래 표현들 중 하나를 더할 수 있습니다.

* Nice!
* Good!
* Great job!
* Well done!

Nice job speaking in a very nice way.
Good kind
Great polite
sweet
thoughtful

오늘 정말 잘했어

시온맘's Pick

"You were fantastic today. You behaved so well."

다양하게 표현할 수 있어요!

You were great (today).
fantastic
awesome

You did a nice job (today).
good
great

* 위 문장들 후에 다음 아래 표현들 중 하나를 더할 수 있습니다.

* You did so well.
* You behaved so well.

사랑스럽구나

시온맘's Pick

"You are such a sweet thing."

다양하게 표현할 수 있어요!

You are (so) lovely.
You are (so) adorable.
You are such a sweet thing.
You are the apple of my eye.

너는 참 특별해

시온맘's Pick

"You are one of a kind."

다양하게 표현할 수 있어요!

* 딸인 경우 Girl, 아들인 경우 Boy.

You are one of a kind.
You are (very) special.
You are a (very) special boy.
girl.

역시 엄마 아들이야
역시 엄마 딸이야

시온맘's Pick

"You are definitely my girl."

다양하게 표현할 수 있어요!

* 딸인 경우 Girl, 아들인 경우 Boy.

That's my boy.
girl.

You are definitely my boy.
girl.

네가 엄마 아들 / 딸이라서 참 좋구나
네가 엄마 아들 / 딸이라서 참 감사해
네가 엄마 아들 / 딸이라서 행복하구나

시온맘's Pick

"I'm grateful to have you as my daughter."

다양하게 표현할 수 있어요!

* 딸인 경우 Daughter, 아들인 경우 Son.

I'm	glad	to have you as my son.
	lucky	daughter.
	happy	
	grateful	

I'm	glad	(that) you are my kid.
	lucky	son.
	happy	child.
	grateful	daughter.

약속 잘 지켜서 예쁘다

시온맘's Pick

"I'm proud of you for keeping your promise."

다양하게 표현할 수 있어요!

I'm glad you kept your promise.
happy

I'm proud of you for keeping your promise.

It makes me very happy to see you keep your promise.

감정 조절의 한계

Setting Limits

(아이의 격한 행동 후)

엄마가 지금 기분이 좋지 않으니, 우리 각자 조금 시간을 갖고 다시 이야기하자구나

시온맘's Pick

"I don't find your behavior acceptable. Mommy would like to be left alone for now. I'm quiet upset. We should talk later."

다양하게 표현할 수 있어요!

* 색깔로 구분하여 나열된 표현들을 (순서에 관계 없이) 하나씩 선택하여 함께 사용하시면, 의미가 전달됩니다.

1) Let's talk later.
   We can
   We should

2) Can we talk a little later?
   Could
   Is it okay if

1) I'm not happy (right now).
2) I'm quite upset (right now).

1) This is not okay.

2) That was not the right thing to do.

3) I don't find your action acceptable.
behavior

4) I'm not happy with what you did.
your actions.
your behavior.

1) Mommy needs to have some time alone.
would like

2) Mommy needs to be left alone (for now).
would like

3) Mommy needs to have some time (right now).
would like

그만 해! 더는 안 되겠다, 그만 하렴

시온맘's Pick

"Mommy said, pack it in."

다양하게 표현할 수 있어요!

(+ I said)
(+ Mommy said)

* 아래 문장들 전이나 후에 "Mommy said" 또는 "I said"를 붙이면 조금 더 단호한 느낌이 날 수 있어요.

Stop it.
Pack it in.
Cut it out.
(That's) Enough.
You've done enough.

* 아래 두 문장은 위에 정리된 표현들과 동일한 뜻을 가지고 있으나, 엄마가 아이에게 쓸 수 있는 표현으로는 적합하지 않습니다.

* I can't take it anymore.
* I can't stand it anymore.

그만 하라고 했지

시온맘's Pick

"I told you to pack it in."

다양하게 표현할 수 있어요!

I told you to stop it.
I told you to cut it out.
I told you to pack it in.
I told you (that's) enough.

엄마 말 들었어?
엄마 말 듣고 있니?

시온맘's Pick

"Can you not hear what I'm saying?"

다양하게 표현할 수 있어요!

Are you with me?
Are you listening (to me)?

Do you hear me?
Did

Did you hear what I said?
Did you not hear what I said?

Do you hear what I'm saying?
Do you not hear what I'm saying?

Can you not hear me?
what I'm saying?

말 안 들으면, 도로 집에 갈 거야

시온맘's Pick

"If you don't behave, I'm going to take you back home."

다양하게 표현할 수 있어요!

If you don't behave, I'll take you back home.
I'm going to

If you don't listen to me, I'll take you back home.
I'm going to

엄마가 몇 번을 말해야 하지?

시온맘's Pick

"How many times do I have to repeat myself?"

다양하게 표현할 수 있어요!

Do I have to repeat myself (again)?

How many times should I tell you?
do I have to

How many times should I repeat myself?
do I have to

엄마가 몇 번을 말했어

시온맘's Pick

"I repeated myself multiple times."

다양하게 표현할 수 있어요!

I told you several times.
multiple
numerous

I repeated myself several times.
multiple
numerous

How many times did I tell you?

I told you (a lot) more than once.

엄마가 말했잖아

시온맘's Pick

"I've already told you."

다양하게 표현할 수 있어요!

I've already said it.
told you.

I (already) said it.
told you.

(정색한 상황)

엄마 얼굴 똑바로 보고 말해보렴

시온맘's Pick

"Then, speak to me. Look straight into my eyes."

다양하게 표현할 수 있어요!

* 색깔로 구분하여 나열된 표현들을 (순서에 관계 없이) 하나씩 선택하여 함께 사용하시면, 의미가 전달됩니다.

1) Look at me.
mommy.

2) Look me in the eyes.
face.

3) Look (directly) into my eyes.
(straight)

4) Look (directly) at my face.
(straight)

1) Now, talk to me.
Then,

2) Now, speak to me.
Then,

3) Now, tell me what you want to say.
Then,

생각의자에 와서 앉아 보렴

시온맘's Pick

"Come and be seated on the time-out chair."

다양하게 표현할 수 있어요!

(+ Please)

Come and sit on the thinking chair.
be seated time-out

Come have a seat on the thinking chair.
take time-out

생각의자에 가서 앉아 있으렴

시온맘's Pick

"You have a seat on the time-out chair."

다양하게 표현할 수 있어요!

(+ Please)

Go to the thinking chair.
time-out

Go sit on the thinking chair.
time-out

Go and have a seat on the thinking chair.
take time-out

(+ Please 안 됨)

You should sit on the thinking chair.
take a seat time-out
have a seat

울어도 소용없단다

시온맘's Pick

"It's no use whining."

다양하게 표현할 수 있어요!

No crying.
whining.

It's no use crying.
whining.

Crying won't work.
Whining

Crying doesn't work.
Whining

Crying is not going to work.
Whining

Crying won't get you anywhere.
Whining

Crying never gets you anywhere.
Whining

소리 지르지 말자

시온맘's Pick

"Keep your voice down, please."

다양하게 표현할 수 있어요!

No yelling.
Stop

No shouting.
Stop

No screaming.
Stop

Don't yell.
shout.
scream.

Keep your voice down.

I want you to stop yelling.
shouting.
screaming.

* 위 문장들 전이나 후에 Please를 더해도 좋습니다.

그만 징징대렴

시온맘's Pick

"I want you to stop being so whiny, please."

다양하게 표현할 수 있어요!

No whining.
Stop

Stop being so whiny.

Stop being (such) a baby.

I want you to stop whining.
being so whiny.
being such a baby.

* 위 문장들 전이나 후에 Please를 더해도 좋습니다.
* Whiny : 투덜대는
* Whine : 징징거리다

그만 골 부리렴

시온맘's Pick

"I want you to stop throwing a fit, please."

다양하게 표현할 수 있어요!

Don't throw a fit.
tantrums.
a tantrum.

Stop throwing a fit.
tantrums.
a tantrum.

I want you to stop throwing a fit.
tantrums.
a tantrum.

* 위 문장들 전이나 후에 Please를 더해도 좋습니다.
* Fit : 흥분, 격발
* Tantrum : 골부림, 성질을 부림

조용히 해, 목소리 조금 낮추렴

시온맘's Pick

"Speak softly, please."

다양하게 표현할 수 있어요!

Be quiet.

Speak softly.

Inside voice!
Indoor voice!

Tone it down.
Keep it down.

Lower your tone.
voice.

* 위 문장들 전이나 후에 Please를 더해 사용할 수 있습니다.

시온맘's Pick

"I'd like for you to **speak softly.**"

이렇게도 표현할 수 있어요!

(+ Could you -?)
(+ I need you to -)
(+ I'd like (for) you to -)
Be quiet.

Speak softly.

Tone it down.
Keep it down.

Lower your tone.
voice.

안 되는 건 안 되는 거야

시온맘's Pick

"When I say, 'No!' I mean it."

다양하게 표현할 수 있어요!

No means no.

When I say, "No!" I mean it.

명심해, 그건 안 되는 거야

시온맘's Pick

"Remember, that's not allowed."

다양하게 표현할 수 있어요!

(+ Please)
Remember, you can't do that.
Remember, that's not allowed.

시온맘's Pick

"Please keep in your mind, that's not allowed."

이렇게도 표현할 수 있어요!

(You must remember)
(You should remember)
(You need to remember)
((+ Please) Keep it in mind)
((+ Please) Keep in your mind)
Remember, you can't do that.
Remember, that's not allowed.

그건 잘못된 거야

시온맘's Pick

"That's not right."

다양하게 표현할 수 있어요!

That's wrong.
That's not right.

반성 좀 해야겠네

시온맘's Pick

"Maybe you need a time-out."

다양하게 표현할 수 있어요!

Maybe you need a time-out.

Maybe you need to sit on a thinking chair.
time-out

왜 이러는 거야?
왜 이렇게 행동하는 거야?
왜 이렇게 고집을 부리는 거니?

시온맘's Pick

"Why is it that you behave like this?"

다양하게 표현할 수 있어요!

Why are you behaving like this?
Why is it that you behave like this?
Why is it that you are behaving like this?

Why are you being (so) stubborn?
Why is it that you are being (so) stubborn?

* Behave : 행동하다
* Stubborn : 고집스러운

그 말 또 하면 혼날 거야
그 말 또 하면 벌 받는 거야

시온맘's Pick

"If you say that again, you will get a time-out."

다양하게 표현할 수 있어요!

If you say that again, I'll punish you.

If you say that again, I'll give you a time-out.
you will get

If you say that again, you'll be in (a) big trouble.

하고 싶은 대로 할 순 없단다
모든 걸 네 마음대로 할 순 없단다

시온맘's Pick

"You can't do exactly as you want all the time."

다양하게 표현할 수 있어요!

You can't do as you please all the time.
things your way

You can't (always) do as you please.
things your way.

It's not always about what you want or want to do.

You can't (always) do (exactly) as you like.
want.

You can't do (exactly) as you like all the time.
want

You can't (always) do whatever you like (to do).
want

You can't do whatever you like (to do) all the time.
want

하기 싫은 것도 해야 할 때가 있단다

시온맘's Pick

"At times, you have to do things you want to avoid."

다양하게 표현할 수 있어요!

At times, you need to do things you want to avoid.
have to / don't want to do.

There are times when you need to do things you want to avoid.
have to / don't want to do.

스스로 할 수 있어야지

시온맘's Pick

"Try to do it on your own."

다양하게 표현할 수 있어요!

(You should) Try to do it yourself.
by yourself.
on your own.

You should be able to do it yourself.
by yourself.
on your own.

엄마가 안 도와줄 거야

시온맘's Pick

"I won't be helping you out."

다양하게 표현할 수 있어요!

I won't help you (out).
give you a hand.

I won't be helping you (out).
giving you a hand.

I'm not going to help you.
give you a hand.

I'm not going to be helping you (out).
giving you a hand.

참을 줄도 알아야지

시온맘's Pick

"You should learn to be patient."

다양하게 표현할 수 있어요!

You should learn to wait.
need to

You should learn to be patient.
need to

이번 한 번만 봐주는 거야

시온맘's Pick

"I'll let it slide only this time."

다양하게 표현할 수 있어요!

I'll let it go (but) only this time.
slide

I'll forgive you (but) only this time.

무엇을 잘못했는지 생각해보렴
네가 한 행동에 대해 생각해보렴

시온맘's Pick

"Think about your own actions."

다양하게 표현할 수 있어요!

Think about your own actions.
Think about what you did (wrong).
Think about what you've done (wrong).

시온맘's Pick

"You should think about your own actions."

이렇게도 표현할 수 있어요!

(+ You should -)
Think about your own actions.
Think about what you did (wrong).
Think about what you've done (wrong).

엄마 이야기 들어보렴

시온맘's Pick

"Please lend an ear to me."

다양하게 표현할 수 있어요!

I need your (close) attention.
need to have

(+ Please)
Listen to me.
Lend me your ears.
Lend an ear to me.
Listen to what I'm saying.
Listen to what I need to say.
have

You should listen to me.
You should listen carefully.
You should pay (close) attention.

시온맘's Pick

"You should **lend an ear to me.**"

이렇게도 표현할 수 있어요!

(+ You should -)

Listen to me.
Lend me your ears.
Lend an ear to me.
Listen to what I'm saying.
Listen to what I need to say.
have

시온맘's Pick

"You have got to **listen carefully.**"

이렇게도 표현할 수 있어요!

(You need to -)
(You'd better -)
(You have got to -)

You should listen to me.
You should listen carefully.
You should pay (close) attention.

엄마 말 좀 들어 말 좀 들어, 말 좀

시온맘's Pick

"Listen to mommy! Will you?"

다양하게 표현할 수 있어요!

* 엄마가 아이에게 자신을 표현하는 경우, 문장의 목적어로 Me, Mom보다는 Mommy를 더 많이 사용합니다. 더 친근한 느낌을 담고 있기 때문입니다.

(+ Please)
Listen! (to me) Will you?
(to mommy)

(감정이 좋지 못한 상태)

엄마 얘기 들어보렴

시온맘's Pick

"Hear me out."

다양하게 표현할 수 있어요!

* 엄마가 아이에게 자신을 표현하는 경우, 문장의 목적어로 Me, Mom보다는 Mommy를 더 많이 사용합니다. 더 친근한 느낌을 담고 있기 때문입니다.

Hear me out.

Listen carefully.

Listen (to me).
(to mommy).

Listen to what I'm saying.

Listen to what I need to say.
have

말대꾸 그만하렴
말대답 그만하렴

시온맘's Pick

"Please **don't give me any of your lip.**"

다양하게 표현할 수 있어요!

(+ Please)

No talking back.

Stop talking back.

Stop answering back (to me).

Don't talk back (to me).

Don't answer back (to me).

Don't give me (no) lip.
(any of your)

듣고 나서 말하렴

시온맘's Pick

"First, you should listen. Then, you can speak."

다양하게 표현할 수 있어요!

(+ Please)

Listen before you talk.
speak.

Listen to me (first) before you start talking.
speaking.

(+ Please 안 됨)

First, you should listen. Then, you can speak.

Before you start talking, (you should) listen to me.
speaking, what I have to say.

엄마 말 좀 끝까지 들었으면 해

시온맘's Pick

"I'd like for you to not interrupt me while I'm talking."

다양하게 표현할 수 있어요!

I'm still talking.

I'm not done (talking) yet.

Could you let me finish (talking)?

I don't want you to interrupt me while I'm talking.
I'd like for you to not

(엄마 말) 명심해

시온맘's Pick

"Mark my words."

다양하게 표현할 수 있어요!

(+ Please)
Mark my words.

Don't forget that.

Keep (it) in mind.
(this)
(that)

Keep (it) in mind. + that 상황 설명.
(this)
(that)

명심해줬으면 좋겠어

시온맘's Pick

"I hope you would keep in mind."

다양하게 표현할 수 있어요!

I want you to not forget it.
would like for you this.
that.

I want you to keep (it) in mind.
would like for you (this)
(that)

I hope (that) you won't forget that.

I hope you (would) keep (it) in mind.
(this)
(that)

공손하게 말해야지

시온맘's Pick

"Please speak in a polite way."

다양하게 표현할 수 있어요!

(+ Please)

Say it politely.
that

Speak politely.

Talk in a polite way.
Speak

Be polite as you talk.
speak.

시온맘's Pick

"You have to speak in a polite way."

이렇게도 표현할 수 있어요!

(+ You should -)
(+ You need to -)
(+ You have to -)
Say it politely.
that

Speak politely.

Talk in a polite way.
Speak

Be polite as you talk.
speak.